Superstar Sales Secrets

By
Barry J. Farber

CAREER PRESS
3 Tice Road
P.O. Box 687
Franklin Lakes, NJ 07417
1-800-CAREER-1
201-848-0310 (outside U.S.)
FAX: 201-848-1727

SUPERSTAR SALES SECRETS

Cover design by A Good Thing, Inc.
Printed in the U.S.A. by Book-mart Press

To order this title, please call toll-free 1-800-CAREER-1 (NJ and Canada: 201-848-0310) to order using VISA or MasterCard, or for further information on books from Career Press.

Library of Congress Cataloging-in-Publication Data

Farber, Barry J.
    Superstar sales secrets / by Barry J. Farber.
      p. cm.
    Includes index.
    ISBN 1-56414-167-5 (pbk.) :
    1. Selling. I. Title.
HF5438.25.F375 1995
658.85--dc20   95-187
                                                CIP

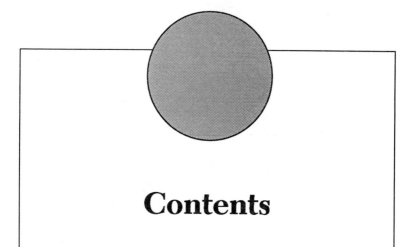

Contents

Introduction   5

Stage 1: Motivation   7

Stage 2: Prospecting   21

Stage 3: Needs analysis   49

Stage 4: Presentations   65

Stage 5: Handling objections   81

Stage 6: Closing   89

Stage 7: Follow-up   95

Stage 8: Time management   101

Index   127

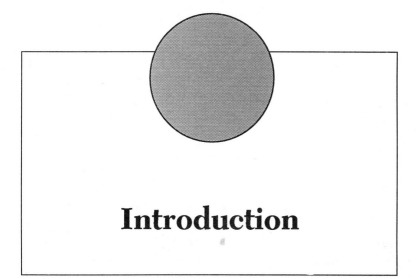

Introduction

The world of sales is not what it used to be. Customers are more sophisticated; they demand not only quality products, but beyond-the-call-of-duty customer service and ongoing relationships as well. Today's sales professionals must demonstrate honesty and integrity, and they must also reach a high level of competency in building rapport and understanding customers' needs. They must have keenly developed questioning techniques, good listening abilities and excellent follow-through.

Included in this book, and in the entire *State of the Art Selling* series, are ideas, tips and techniques researched from several sources: from high-performance, award-winning salespeople across the country; from extraordinarily successful people in a variety of professions; and, most importantly, from customers who have expressed what they need and want most from a top sales performer.

The goal of this book is to provide a practical outline of the stages of the sales cycle, along with tools and techniques to help you go through them. It focuses on the basics of sales success. In that sense, it's perfect for beginners who need step-by-step guidelines. But it's also geared toward the seasoned professional who may be stalled or in a slump; this book offers a return-to-the-basics approach to get you back on track.

You won't find any manipulative sales techniques here, nor a thousand-and-one ways to close a sale. You will find real-world, results-oriented suggestions that will get you started (or re-started) on the road to success and help you through any hardships all salespeople experience at one time or another.

Special thanks to all the superstar sales reps and managers who gave their time and shared their insights.

Special thanks to the Career Press staff: to Ron Fry and Larry Wood for their support, enthusiasm and publishing excellence; and to Betsy Sheldon, Ellen Scher, Regina McAloney and Sue Gruber for their outstanding work and quality in production.

And to Sharyn Kolberg with great appreciation for her patient listening and her excellent editorial skills.

Stage
1

Motivation

Nobody ever said selling was easy. It takes hard work and persistence to do it well and achieve success. Rejection and adversity are daily occurrences in this profession. That's why motivation is the most important factor in sales success.

There's an old saying that goes, "Life is like a grindstone—it either grinds you down or polishes you up." You can let rejection and adversity grind you down. Or you can face up to hardship and view it as an opportunity and challenge that can spur you on to greater success.

Why is it that two salespeople of equal talent and ability don't always achieve equal success? How is it that some people, whether they're selling products or services, paper clips or pharmaceuticals, can rise above rejection, hardship and failure? What is the common denominator that puts these people in the category called "successful"?

The strongest link between all these people is summed up in one word—attitude: attitude towards your job, your company, your product and your customers. One Harvard Business School study determined that there are four factors critical to sales success: information, intelligence, skill and attitude. When these factors were ranked by importance, this particular study found that information, intelligence and skill combined amounted to seven percent of sales effectiveness—and attitude amounts to 93 percent! Could it be that 93 percent of our success in sales, at work and in life results from our attitude?

A positive attitude is critical in sales. A prospect mirrors a salesperson's attitudes and expectations. If the salesperson does not expect the prospect to buy, she creates doubt and negative expectations in the prospect. Here are some keys for developing the magical attitude of positive expectation:

A positive attitude is the expectation that if we do all that we can do, if we develop our potential to its fullest, we will achieve the results we want.

Eight keys to a positive attitude

1. **Enthusiasm.** Enthusiasm is the great equalizer. It can help us overcome obstacles and can often make up for deficiencies or lack of skill in a particular area. There are two steps necessary to keep enthusiasm going:

    - Learning as much as possible before we take action.
    - Reviewing and remembering our accomplishments and successes.

2. **Focus on the positive.** In any negative situation, failure or setback, look for the good that comes out of it and for what you can do differently next time.

3. **Professional pride.** As we develop more and more complex products and services, it takes the assistance of highly trained, motivated salespeople to help customers determine which product or service meets their needs. Your efforts as a salesperson are only rewarded if you are fully engaged and totally immersed in your craft. Think of yourself as a consultant. Top salespeople proudly refer

to themselves as sales professionals. Until you feel pride in your profession, you cannot develop the powerful, positive attitude that leads to sales stardom.

4. **Invest in your profession.** You have to invest time, energy and enthusiasm to develop mastery of your skill. In order to stay 100 percent invested, you must have something at stake—your self-esteem, money, reputation, the well-being of your family—anything that's important to you. Once you've invested in the process of sales, you're rewarded for the accomplishment of your goals. Your reward might be the sense of accomplishment that comes with a successful close, a fat commission check or the respect and admiration of your peers. Whatever the reward, you believe that you are doing the right thing for yourself and your customers.

5. **Invest in yourself.** The most important asset you have as a salesperson is yourself. You must continually upgrade your product knowledge, understanding of the industry, understanding of your customers and sales skills. The top sales stars take advantage of every training opportunity they have, listening to tapes and reading books on positive thinking, sales techniques and psychology.

6. **Positive persistence.** Top salespeople are extremely persistent, but they find positive ways of being persistent. It's more than just showing up on someone's doorstep day after day and saying, "Are you ready?" The stars always have a reason for a call, whether it's new information about the product or service or an article they think the customer might be interested in. However, one of

the toughest decisions for a salesperson to make is when to stop pursuing a customer. Eventually you develop an instinct for when a prospect is truly interested or qualified.

7. **Surround yourself with the markers of success.** Keep track of (and display) key achievements or goals or anything that can help you focus on the positive when things get tough. Keeping your goals in sight, literally and figuratively, fuels the fire of motivation.

8. **Learn from failure.** This is the most important key. Sales is one profession where failure is a daily reality. If you want to succeed, have the courage to fail and learn from your mistakes. Failure isn't failure if we discover its lessons.

Practicing a positive attitude

It doesn't take years of hard work or mystical experiences to develop a positive attitude. It takes practice. People react to the way you approach them. If you're annoyed and upset with the world, you'll surely find that people are annoyed and upset with you. If you're warm and open, you'll find people will be that way with you. However, even if people don't react the way you'd like them to, it's your responsibility to maintain a good attitude. Here are some tips for developing and maintaining a positive attitude:

✓ **Start every morning on a positive note.** For 15 minutes, read or listen to a positive message from the motivational or self-help field. Or broaden your product knowledge and stay up-to-date on your field by reading educational materials.

✓ **Tape the word "attitude" to your bathroom mirror**, in your car or wherever you can look at it every single day. Realize that your success is determined more by your attitude than anything else.

✓ **Avoid negative people and attitudes.** If people around you are gossiping or focusing on the negative, change the subject or walk away. If you have nothing good to say, don't say anything.

✓ **Take a positive physical approach.** Clean out your system for 30 days: exercise regularly and stay away from excess caffeine, alcohol, tobacco and fatty foods.

✓ **Keep a diary of all the positive events that happen every day.** What did you do well today? What did you accomplish? Write down any compliments or praise you received. Nothing is too small or trivial to be included. Review the diary at the end of each week.

✓ **Make everyone you meet glad that she met you.** Picture everyone you meet with the words "make me feel important" on their foreheads.

Debunking the myth of the overnight success

When we see an athlete win a game or a politician win a race, or any top achiever reach a pinnacle of success, all we see is the end result. We don't see the investment of blood, sweat and tears that came before the accolades and recognition. So we tend to think that peak performers have an easy time of it, and we're the only ones who have to struggle to reach our goals. Of course, this is not true; there are no get-rich-quick success secrets. However, there are some things you can do to increase your chances for success:

✓ **Give 100 percent all the time.** After every endeavor, ask yourself, "Did I give it my best?" William H. Danforth (founder of Ralston Purina and author of the inspirational book *I Dare You!*) used this motto for living a better life: "To be our own selves, at our very best, all the time." Knowing you put in your best at work also allows you guilt-free enjoyment of your leisure time.

✓ **Realize that it is not luck that makes a person successful.** People who are "lucky" are those who are prepared when an opportunity presents itself. Luck happens when you're learning, when you're working harder than the next person, when you're putting in that extra effort. Some people see luck in others' positive outcomes. But luck really lies in hard work and extraordinary effort.

✓ **Practice resistance-training for the brain.** When you're doing something that's tough and painful, remember that we resist most things that build us most. It's these experiences that help us when we're suddenly hit by an obstacle. We have built our substance and stamina through the resistance-training. It's getting through the tough steps and stages that builds character, not going over the finish line.

Surround yourself with positive role models

The road to success doesn't have to be barren and lonely. There are people everywhere who are willing to help if we are willing to ask. High achievers are constantly studying other people and their methods of accomplishment. They surround themselves, not only with markers of their own success, but with models of others' successes as well. Here are some ways you can do the same:

✓ **Make careful choices about whom you wish to follow.** Don't play follow-the-follower, a lonely and potentially dangerous game. Look for people whose values match your own and who have achieved excellence in their field.

✓ **Surround yourself with models of success.** Choose your mentors carefully. Learn to ask for help and support, and learn how to find resources for getting the help you need. If you surround yourself with positive images, you will find yourself moving in positive directions.

✓ **Keep your ears, heart and mind open.** There are many people around who are willing to teach us. It's sometimes easier for others to see things we are unable to see, so don't dismiss someone's advice or opinions without first giving them careful study.

✓ **Expose yourself to a variety of new and challenging situations.** Network constantly. You never know who, out of all the people you meet, will be the one who can help you achieve your goals.

✓ **Look to yourself to be your greatest mentor.** Choose your influences and your surroundings as you wish your life to be. You become what you think about.

"Your living is determined not so much by what life brings to you as by the attitude you bring to life; not so much by what happens as by the way your mind looks at what happens."

John Homer Miller

Positive attitude checklist

1. Enthusiasm.
2. Focus on the positive.
3. Develop professional pride.
4. Invest in your profession.
5. Invest in yourself.
6. Develop positive persistence.
7. Surround yourself with markers of success.
8. Learn from failure. *Platinum Rule* ✶

✓ **Remember the Golden Rule.** Treat others as you would like to be treated. It sounds simple, but it works. If you approach people in a warm and open manner, most respond in kind.

✓ **Practice, practice, practice.** It's not always easy to maintain a positive attitude when outside circumstances pull us down. But if you

✶ Treat others how they want to be treated — harder to do but far more effective !

work at having a positive attitude every day, you will have reserves to carry you through the rough times.

✓ **Keep track of your own achievements.** We all experience personal and professional triumphs—large and small—every day. Constantly remind yourself of the things that went well. Write them down, and keep them in sight.

Facing fear and failure

Henry Ford once said, "One who fears limits his activities. Failure is only the opportunity to more intelligently begin again." Some of life's greatest lessons are taught through hardships, failure, fear and mistakes. The most successful people learn to overcome obstacles, confront fear and turn it into a motivating force, and take action in the face of adversity. Here are some tips on how you, too, can deal with fear and failure:

✓ **Use failure as the ultimate learning tool.** Every disappointment teaches a positive lesson—you just have to look for it. If you make the same mistakes over and over again and don't learn anything from them, then you have failed. It is in times of adversity that we grow the most.

✓ **Success is our greatest revenge.** When people are discouraging or critical, ask yourself, "Who are they to judge me?" and tell yourself, "I'll prove them wrong." This is a great source of energy and a motivator to push you into action.

henceforth shall be referred to as "A Invaluable lesson"

Motivation

Invaluable Lesson.

✓ **Once you perceive a problem or an obstacle, learn from it as quickly as you can and then move on.** If you've made a mistake, understand that you'll do it differently next time. Dwelling on failure only causes you to fail again.

Remember This

✓ **FEAR is an acronym for False Evidence Appearing Real.** Therefore, the first step in taming fear is to analyze what is real and what is not. Then dive in and take action. Fear is what you imagine it to be. When you attack it, you diminish it.

✓ **Preparation and action are the greatest combatants of fear.** The only way to conquer fear is to study it and prepare in every possible way. Learn all about your product or service. Learn as much as you can about your customer's business. Study sales techniques; look to the top people in your company or industry and study their attitudes and sales methods. Reduce fear by increasing your knowledge and focusing your nervous energy on preparation, instead of allowing it to fuel your imagination.

Common sales pitfalls

There are many things you can do to sabotage your sales success. Here are 10 of them:

1. Don't plan. *Do not know script!*
2. Don't spend enough time prospecting.
3. Lead with price.

---

4. Never have enough detailed information on the customer.

5. Be impatient.

6. Go into your presentation too early.

7. Overcommit yourself.

8. Fail to understand the decision-making process.

9. Talk too much—listen too little. *—Best Listeners*

10. Don't follow-through. *are always Considered Most Knowledgeable*

Key success factors from top performers

On the other hand, there are many things you can do to increase your chances of sales success. Here are some of the factors necessary for success, gathered from top performers in all areas of sales:

1. Enthusiasm.

2. Effort.

3. Always be available.

4. Do the little things (go beyond customers' expectations.)

5. Professionalism (pride in profession.)

6. Know your customer's business.

7. Listen—Listen—Listen! *— Most Knowledgeable sales person per Client!*

8. Have a sense of humor.

9. Set goals.

10. Follow-up.

11. Always be prospecting.

12. Never stop learning.

13. Learn from the top performers.

14. Build long-term customer relationships.

15. Use a low-pressure approach.

16. Differentiate yourself through superior service.

17. Start and end with a positive attitude.

> *"If you do what you've always done, you'll get what you've always gotten."*
>
> Anonymous

Motivation checklist

✓ **Turn fear and failure into a motivating force.** Learn from your mistakes. Challenge yourself to do better next time.

✓ **Use others' criticisms as a source of energy.** If the criticism is constructive, learn what you can from it and move on. If not, use it to spur you on to greater achievement.

✓ **Don't dwell on the past.** Think of how you can improve today by using what you learned yesterday.

✓ **Prepare yourself and take action.** Inaction breeds depression. Conquer your fears by

---

preparing as much as possible and taking necessary actions. *Know Script!*

✓ **Beware of self-sabotage.** Review the common sales pitfalls on page 17, and learn to avoid them.

✓ **Learn from the success of others.** Study the key success factors on page 18. Find people in your company who have achieved success, and ask them what unique methods they've used. Ask them if they'll help you learn. Most people will be glad to share their knowledge and experience.

✓ **You become what you think about.** Use your mind to visualize future events. Focus on a successful outcome. Mentally rehearse any new job or task as you physically practice it, and you are preparing for success.

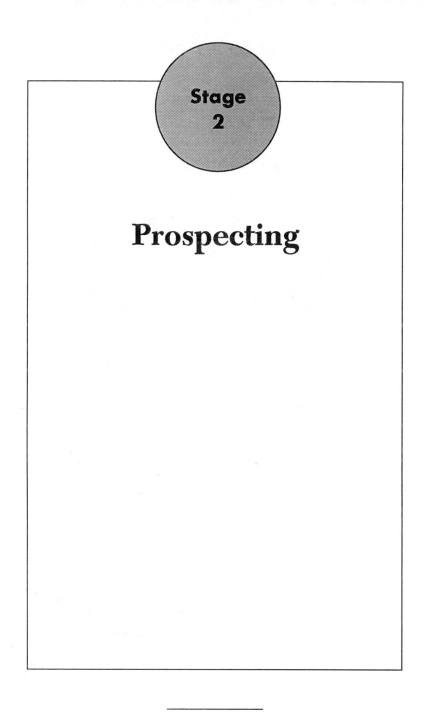

**Stage
2**

Prospecting

Johnny Appleseed had the right idea. Everywhere he went, he scattered seeds all around him. He knew that some seeds would take root and grow, but many would not. Yet that didn't discourage him. In fact, it gave him incentive to sow more seeds, knowing that more would take root, and eventually the whole country would enjoy the fruits of his labor.

Prospecting is based on the Johnny Appleseed principal: If you are prospecting all the time, your chances of reaping rewards are greater. There are eight keys to successful prospecting:

1. **Always be prospecting.** Plant so many seeds that you don't have to worry about each individual sale. You have much more confidence when you know that if one sale falls through, another will sprout in its place. Constant prospecting gives you the experience needed to gain confidence.

2. **Qualify your prospecting activity.** Target key customers who have the greatest ability to buy your product or service.

3. **Build relationships.** Treat prospects as if they are already your best customers.

4. **Understand that rejection comes with the territory.** Nobody likes rejection, but there is one basic truth in selling: If you're not getting a lot of rejections, you're not working hard enough.

Invaluable Lessons

5. **Learn from your mistakes.** You're bound to make some along the way; ask yourself what you can do differently next time.

6. **Believe 110 percent in your product or service.** If you believe that your product or service can help people solve their problems and make their lives a little easier, then you'll want to be out there selling all the time.

7. **Keep an organized list of who to call.** Use research, networking and referrals to increase your chances of success.

8. **Don't be afraid to move on.** Make sure you're not wasting time with people who are stalling or leading you on. If you have enough other activity, you don't need "going-nowhere" accounts.

Successful selling is not a 9-to-5 job. Top salespeople are prospecting all the time. The more you put into your sales career, the more you get out of it.

> *Opportunity is missed by most people because it is dressed in overalls and looks like work.*
>
> Thomas Edison

Your sales goal is to attract and maintain customers—in other words, to build relationships. Every time you meet someone, you should be sincerely interested in learning about who they are, what they do and whether or not you can be of service to them. Never push yourself on people; that only pushes them away. Customers are too intelligent to fall for manipulative tricks. But they will respond to a sincere desire to find out how your product or service can be of benefit to them. Here are several techniques you can use to make your prospecting positive and productive.

Successful cold calling

The ultimate goal of any sales call is, of course, to get the business. But most sales are not as simple as "Hi, I'm here to sell you something; sign on the dotted line." A sale usually consists of several steps, the first of which may be the cold call.

The goal of a cold call is to gather information—to find out if there is an opportunity at this account. If this account seems promising, you move on to the next stage in your sales cycle. There are several key ideas to keep in mind when cold calling:

✓ **Start early and stay late.** If you think you've heard this before, you have. But it's often the best way get into a company, because the "gatekeeper" has not yet arrived, or has gone for the day. If you walk in at 5:30 p.m., you just might run into a sales manager, or even the business owner. They'll appreciate the fact that you're working after normal business hours; therefore you've already got one factor working in your favor—credibility. And they may have more time to see you than they would during normal business hours.

✓ **No matter who you see at the front door, try to make them smile.** A little humor (always in a professional manner) goes a long way. You want the person you're meeting to feel comfortable with you. Some smile-producing entrances include:

• When asked, "Do you have an appointment?" reply with "No. I'm a pleasant surprise!"

- Introduce yourself and say, "I know you make all the decisions in this office, but can I speak to the person who *thinks* they make all the decisions?"

✓ **Introduce yourself, and try to get the other person to do the same.** As soon as you make someone smile, say, "Hi. I'm John Doe. I'm glad I got you to smile." Usually the person will answer, "Hello. I'm Susan." Then you can continue with, "Susan, I wonder if you could help me out?" Try and use the person's name as much as possible. The next step is to ask, "Is the owner in?" or, "What's the name of the president of the company, and how do I contact him?" or, "Who is the person that makes the decisions on (your type of product or service)?"

✓ **Practice top-down selling.** Start the sales process with the head of the company. Call the office of the president. Even if you don't get to speak to that person, you'll probably get to his or her assistant, who can usually give you valuable information about the company. Ask the assistant to direct you to the person who handles the purchase of your type of product or service. When the assistant says, "Bob Jones handles that," you can call Bob Jones, say that you've just been speaking with the president's office, and it was recommended that you speak with him. It's much harder to work your way up through the company and go over people's heads to get to the next level. Selling from the top down is a good way to establish relationships with high-level people in the company.

✓ **Don't judge a company by its facade.** There are three reasons for this: 1. The size of a company's office doesn't always relate to the size of its bottom line; 2. Other sales reps are probably passing this company by; and 3. Even if they can't use your services, they may be able to recommend you to people who can.

✓ **After you've gathered as much information as possible, try to make an appointment.** If this is not immediately possible, get back in touch by phone. Make notes about everyone you spoke to and everything that happened during the cold call so that you can refer back to them. For instance, you might say, "Hi, Susan. This is John Doe. I came in the other day as the pleasant surprise. Remember me?" This is what will differentiate you from the dozens of other salespeople this person has talked to recently.

✓ **Make people feel important.** Ask targeted questions, and get them to open up. Listen for what's important to them.

✓ **Every time you leave a cold call, ask this question:** "Do you know of anybody else in the area who could benefit from our products or services?"

Cold calling checklist

✓ **Treat everyone equally.** No matter who you meet at the front door, give them the same respect you would give the owner of the company. Not only is that the polite thing to do, you never know how much power they have. If you alienate the person at the front desk, you may never get in. On the other hand, if you make a friend, you may succeed where others have failed.

✓ **Diffuse objections. Get as much information as possible, even if there is no present need for your product or service.** Never get defensive. Your goal is to gather information in a way that makes the customer feel comfortable about giving it. If there is no present need, you can say, "I can appreciate that. But perhaps in the future you might need to change vendors. If I have a better understanding of your business and how it operates, I may be able to help you at that time. By the way, what type of system are using now?" You could also handle the situation by saying, "I don't want to sell you something you just bought. But if your needs change, or if we have opportunities to help you in other areas, I'd like to have a better understanding of how I might be able to help you. What type of system did you just buy?"

✓ **Ask for written information about the company.** Pick up brochures, annual reports or any other written information that will give you insights you can use when you follow-up with a phone call to the company.

✓ **Be yourself.** You're not just a salesperson; you're a human being with a unique style and personality. Find your own ways to use humor, make friends and allies, and differentiate yourself from the competition.

Telemarketing techniques

For many salespeople, telemarketing is the most difficult part of selling. It's much easier for a customer to turn you down over the phone than it is when you're face-to-face. You may feel that you're interrupting someone's valuable time; but your time is valuable as well, and you're calling with something of genuine value to the potential customer.

Often, you will have to speak to a gatekeeper before you get through to the decision-maker. Never look upon this person as your enemy. Once again, treat everyone equally. You have a job to do; gatekeepers are trying to do theirs. One way of handling this is to say, "Hi. Can you put me through to Jane Smith please?" They might say, "Who's calling?" You can say, "This is John Doe from ABC Company. Can you put me through please?" You've answered their question, and then asked again to put you through.

The next question you're often asked is, "What is this in regard to?" If you try to manipulate or mislead the gatekeeper, they'll see right through it—and remember you for it. Think about a benefit you've provided to others and how it might apply to this company. Your response could be:

- "It's regarding increased efficiency ideas for your office. Can you put me through please?"

- "It's regarding information that was mailed out to her. Can you put me through please?"

- "It's regarding increasing your market share 15 to 20 percent. Can you put me through please?"

- You don't have to explain what you do for a living. You want to get through to the decision-maker.

When you do get through to the decision-maker, the object of the call is to begin a relationship. Why should someone who doesn't know you at all, who can't see your face, buy from you? They won't, unless you let them know who you are, why you're calling and what you can do for them. Successful telemarketing is a three-step process:

1. **Introduction.** Nobody likes to get a call and not know who they're talking to. Tell them who you are, who you work for and what you're selling.

2. **Benefit statements.** Let your customer know how you've helped others, and how you can do the same for them. If possible, mention the name of a company the customer is familiar with. For example, you could say, "I've been working with Acme Button Company in your town. I helped them increase their sales volume and decrease costs in the area of..." Mention several of the benefits your product or service provided for Acme and can provide for this customer as well.

3. **Close for the appointment.** Follow the benefit statement by requesting an appointment. One of the following approaches may work for you:

   - "I'd like to have the opportunity to do the same for you. How's next Tuesday at 10:20 a.m.?"

   - "I'd like to share 10 or 15 minutes with you next Tuesday to see if we can do the same for you. Is 10:20 a.m. good for you?"

- Remember, you're sharing the time with the customer, not taking it from him. And most people don't have appointments at odd times such as 10:20 a.m. or 3:50 p.m.

- Everything that happens during a telemarketing call should lead towards your ultimate goal: laying the foundation for a solid relationship with that client.

Telemarketing checklist

✓ **Plan and strategize.** Do your homework before you pick up the phone. Do you know who you're calling? Are you clear about your objectives? Do you know what action you want the customer to take at the end of this call—make an appointment, give you information, provide a reference, close the sale?

✓ **Let the customer know who you are and why you're calling.** You want customers to be paying attention to the way in which you can help. You don't want them to spend the time wondering who you are and why you're wasting their time.

✓ **Don't just "send some literature."** A lot of potential customers will ask to see something in writing before they go further with the sale. If you're trying to set up a face-to-face appointment, you might say something like, "We have a number of products and services.

What I'd really like to do is get together with you and find our what your needs are, so that I can recommend what's best for you. Is Tuesday morning good, or is the afternoon better for you?" Or, you can just say, "I prefer to get together instead. Is Tuesday morning good..."

Sometimes you can't avoid sending out materials. If you do, include more than just a note saying, "Here's the literature you requested." Customize your letter so that you reiterate the important points covered in your conversation. The letter below is typical of one I send out following a cold call:

Dear Steve,

Thanks again for your time on the phone the other day, and congratulations on your new product launch. Enclosed is the information you requested, which includes a brochure on our company and some of the products we have available.

Also enclosed are testimonials from customers in businesses similar to yours about the benefits they've received in working with us.

If you have any questions, please don't hesitate to call. I'll be following up with you on Tuesday, Sept. 20 to set up a time for us to meet, so that I can find out more about your key needs and how we can be of benefit to your organization.

Once again, thank you for your time and interest. I look forward to speaking with you soon.

Sincerely,

John Doe

John J. Doe

✓ **Let the customer know you wouldn't be calling unless you had something valuable to share.** If the prospect says, "I'm really not interested right now," you can say, "Ms. Smith, I'll tell you what. If I can't show you ways to add tremendous value to your organization, I will never, ever call you again. I'd love to share just 10 minutes with you to show what kind of benefits we've provided to other customers." If the customer still insists she doesn't have the time or interest, say "Thank you for your time," and let it go.

✓ **Answer objections with the "feel, felt, found" formula.** Typical objections you'll hear include: "I'm not interested." "I don't have time right now." I just bought one." "We're happy with our present vendor." "My brother-in-law is in the business." There's no point in arguing with customers—as soon as you argue, you lose. What you can say is, "I understand how you feel." You're creating empathy with the customer, rather than arguing or getting defensive. The next step is to use the success of your present customers. "A lot of my present customers felt the same way. But when they found out how much time they saved by using our product, they were amazed. Why don't we get together to find out if we can do the same for you. Is Tuesday morning good, or would the afternoon be better?" This is a non-manipulative, non-aggressive way to deal with an objection.

✓ **Stand up while you're talking on the phone.** When you stand, you give your diaphragm room to expand, and your voice should be stronger and clearer. If you sit in one spot all day making calls, you're bound to run out of energy quickly. Stand up. Walk around if you can. Your increased energy will come across in your tone of voice and manner of speaking.

✓ **Give yourself feedback.** It's perfectly legal to tape your own phone conversations, as long as it's for training purposes. When the call is over, play the tape back and evaluate your approach, how you built the relationship, how you handled objections, how you closed and how you sound in general.

✓ **Call early and call late.** The best times for telemarketing are 8 to 9 a.m. and 5 to 6 p.m. You can often catch the decision-maker without having to go past the gatekeeper.

Unique methods of networking

Salespeople are natural-born networkers. If we didn't truly enjoy connecting with people, we wouldn't stay in sales very long. That doesn't mean that networking comes easily to all salespeople. It's both a skill and an art, and it takes practice to make it work for you.

The idea behind networking is that people make mutually beneficial contacts. You can go to a meeting and hand out business cards to everyone you meet. That's not networking. The best method is to forget about your own agenda and find out about the other person's. Then you can determine whether or not the person is a potential prospect and figure out how best to present your ideas.

Networking is when you gather information about someone (who he is, what he does, his needs, his interests, his problems,) and you give out information about yourself (who you are, what you do, what differentiates you from others in your field.) From those beginnings you develop relationships that logically lead to sales. Here are several suggestions for effective networking:

- ✓ **Applaud people for their achievements.** Most people are motivated by recognition, so why not motivate them to get to know you by recognizing their achievements. Study industry newsletters and magazines, as well as your local paper, for announcements of awards, new hires and promotions. Cut the article out of the paper and send it to the person with a note or a card saying, "Congratulations on your new promotion. I wish you continued success and look forward to speaking with you." When you call to follow up, nine times out of 10 they'll take your call, and a relationship can begin.

- ✓ **Use customers' business cards as reference guides.** When you get a business card from a potential customer, don't just file it away and forget about it. Write on it everything you know about the customer—hobbies, interests, birthday, spouse's name, names of children, etc.—anything you might want to refer to in later conversations. You make the customer feel special when you take the trouble to remember personal information; and when you have it written down on the card, you don't have to depend on your own, sometimes faulty, memory.

- ✓ **Send announcement cards.** This is a very useful practice that started in the real estate industry. When an agent sold a house, she would send out announcement cards to all the houses in the neighborhood, announcing "Another house sold by Nancy Smith." If anyone else was interested in selling, they would know who to contact. When you make a sale, send out a card that says, "Announcing..." on the front flap. When you open the card, it reads:

> Another ACE Computer System installation
> At _____ On _____
> By: Acme Office Machines, NY, NY
> (212) 555-1234

Then follow up with a phone call saying, "I recently sent you an announcement of our installation at XYZ Company and wanted to find out how we could be of similar benefit to you."

✓ **Send thank-you notes to people who *don't* buy from you.** No matter how good a salesperson you are, you're not going to make every sale. But you can turn a meeting into a potential relationship by sending a thank-you note anyway. Here's a sample:

Dear Steve,

Thanks again for allowing me to come and spend some time to learn about your needs and find out about your products. I understand that you've chosen to deal with another vendor at this time. I wish you success in all your goals. If you have any questions in the future, or if I can help you in any way, please don't hesitate to call.

A letter like this leaves the door open. Many times, the customer ends up calling because the vendor they went with made promises they couldn't keep. When that vendor doesn't work out, they can't help but think of the salesperson who took the time to send a thank-you note—especially when they didn't get one from the people who did get their business.

✓ **Be a joiner.** One of the best ways to meet prospective customers is to join civic and non-profit organizations. Find a cause that sincerely interests you and you can kill two birds with one stone: while you're networking with other members, you're also doing good deeds.

✓ **Go beyond what the customer expects.** You can establish long-term relationships by going beyond sales-related activities. For instance, a sales rep at Mallinckrodt Veterinary recently had a customer who was moving into a new office. The rep took his own weekend time to help the vet move. This accomplished three things: 1) He got to know his customer's business from an insider's viewpoint; 2) He established himself as someone who cares about his customers and is not just pushing a product; and 3) He no longer has to stop at the desk and say, "Can I see the doctor?" He walks right through to see the vet. He has made a long-term customer who will see him anytime.

✓ **Focus on helping others** get what they want, and in the end, you'll get what you want, too.

Networking checklist

- ✓ **Let people know who you are.** It's not enough to get to know other people—you have to let them know who you are as well. Let them know what makes you special, what differentiates you from the competition, and why they should do business with you.

- ✓ **Never underestimate the power of a thank-you.** Send thank-you notes to people who give you referrals—whether or not they pan out. Show your appreciation, and they may be willing to give you other referrals down the line.

- ✓ **Always do the best job you can.** Word of mouth is the best networking tool ever invented. If you serve your customers well, they'll make connections for you.

- ✓ **The purpose of networking is not only to get sales—it's to build relationships.** In any solid relationship, there is a natural desire for the parties involved to help each other. People you network with know that you're a salesperson and that you would like to make a sale. If they think this is your only interest in them, they may be reluctant to buy. They'd rather deal with someone who is genuinely interested in them, and who will help them solve their problems. If you build a relationship on trust and caring, you will also eventually build a sale.

Prospecting from your customer base

Every sales book written will tell you that it's easier to keep a customer you have than to get a new one. However, many salespeople get so caught up in the "excitement of the chase"—the pursuit of new clients—that they forget about the client base they already have. You want to do more than just keep your current clients; you want to expand the amount of business you're doing with them.

It takes work to keep any relationship going and growing. You can't depend on your product to keep your customers loyal. Nowadays, there's so much product parity that if you want to keep the competitive edge, you've got to provide the one thing your customers can't get from anyone else—personalized service. Your present customers can be the best source of future business. Here are some suggestions for prospecting from your customer base:

- ✓ **Make personal contact a priority.** Keep your 10 best customers on speed dial so that you can call them when you have a free moment to say hello. This serves as a constant reminder of who your key contacts are and that you should keep in touch. With the press of one button, you can call to say hello, find out what's new with their business and see if there's any way you can be of further service.

- ✓ **Keep your customers in mind.** If you see an article in a newspaper or magazine that might be of interest to them, send it to them. It could be some relevant industry news (theirs or yours), or it could be something related to a sport or hobby that interests them.

✓ **Follow your MAP.** Use your MAP board to keep track of customers' buying cycles. Then send out mailings to them every three, six or twelve months (or whatever their cycle is) announcing a new product or development, or to find out if there's any way you can be of service. (See page 114 for MAP explanation.)

✓ **Implement customer satisfaction surveys.** Many customers who have minor complaints will never say anything about them—they just won't buy from you again. If you ask them for their opinion, however, they'll be glad to tell you, and most often they'll be glad to give you the chance to solve the problem. Call your customers and ask, "Is there anything we're not doing we should be doing?" Or, every few months, send current customers a one-page survey about how you and your product or service are performing. The survey has two functions: it gives you a chance to correct any problems, and it can be used as a selling tool for prospective clients. A positive survey from a satisfied customer reassures a prospect that he, too, can expect satisfaction.

✓ **Build a reputation as a problem-solver.** Problems are opportunities. Research conducted by the United States Office of Consumer Affairs showed that of consumers who complain and receive a satisfactory response, 70 percent become the company's most loyal customers. If you should receive a complaint, go beyond the customer's expectations in solving the problem.

✓ **Learn about your customer's business, and think of ways to help their business grow.** Help your customers in any way you can—whether or not it has anything to do with sales. You might run into someone who could benefit from your customer's product or service. You might be in a position to help get your customer some publicity or have some promotion ideas. Whatever you can do to help your customer's business will help yours as well.

✓ **Remember that customers buy from people they *like*, *trust*, and *respect*.**

Like. A customer doesn't necessarily want to become your friend, but she does want to feel comfortable with you. She has to feel a connection with you. She wants to know that you are being yourself and that you can listen and respond to her needs.

Trust. Trust is the basis for all sales relationships—especially those that entail ongoing and long-term sales cycles. TRUST is an acronym for the critical elements of a strong relationship:

Truth.	Be totally honest.
Reliability.	Never promise something you can't deliver.
Uncommon effort.	Go the extra step to earn the business.
Service.	Superb service builds trust.
Truth.	Openness and honesty, start to finish.

40

Respect. Customers will respect you when you are knowledgeable about your product or service and when you're prepared and professional on your calls. But they'll respect you even more when you take time to learn their business and their needs, and show your commitment to helping them achieve their goals.

Tips to keep customers coming back

Top sales performers measure their success not only by the quantity of sales they make, but by their quality as well. Obviously, high achievers in sales keep their customers coming back again and again. The following list of practical tips and ideas has not been devised from some textbook or theoretical practice. This information—which you've read about before in this section, but is well worth repeating—has been applied by hundreds of top achievers and successful businesses throughout the country.

✓ **Attitude and enthusiasm.** These two principles have been the basis for more sales success than any other factors. Enthusiasm comes from the Greek word "entheos" which means "the god within." Isn't that an apt description? Think back to times when you've been enthusiastic about something. Didn't it make you feel good? Empowered? Spirited? As if the "god within" was giving your life a lift? Enthusiasm can often carry us far beyond any skill or talent we may be lacking. In many instances, we can supersede our deficiencies by turning on an engine of enthusiasm. Attitude often determines our altitude in life. Having a positive attitude towards a situation determines more of an outcome than any other factor involved in success. With a great attitude, we usually can control 95 percent of what happens to us, with the other 5 percent that is uncontrollable based on outside sources. Remember, most people will react to you in the exact way you approach them. For example, if you are enthusiastic and excited to see someone, you'll usually get the same type of response. This is called "mirroring." The world around us is a reflection of our attitude toward our environment.

✓ **Differentiation.** What makes you unique as a salesperson? What makes a customer come back to you again and again, and refer other people to you? When someone buys from you, they must feel as if they received tremendous value for what they bought; they must also remember something unique about you because you separated yourself from the competition. One top professional took photographs of each of his customers. He mailed a copy to the customer with a note that said, "Here's looking at you! Thanks again for your business." This small personal touch made this salesperson a definite standout.

✓ **Know your customer's business as well as you know your own.** Ask qualifying questions to find out as much as you can about your customer's company. Study the industry in which he's involved. Find out who his customers are. When you care about a customer's business, he knows you're not just trying to push a product down his throat. He'll value your opinion as well as your product or service.

✓ **Follow-up and feedback.** One of the most important areas of business today is not the first sale, but the consistent repeat business we get after the sale. You can follow-up after the sale by phone, in person or through direct mail. Let them know you appreciate the sale and are available for questions or problems. You not only help your customers that way, but you get them to recommend you to others.

✓ **Effective referrals.** People who are satisfied with your product and service become extremely loyal customers. They're the best method of advertising you'll ever find. Give them incentives to refer others to you. Why not give a discount or a free gift with each referral? Use every contact with your customer to ask, "Do you know anyone else who might benefit from what I have to offer?"

Customer-based prospecting checklist

✓ **Ask your customers for feedback.** Find out what you're doing right and what you're doing wrong. If there are problems, find ways to fix them. Ask your customer what you need to do to maintain and increase their business with you.

✓ **Deliver on everything you promise.** Better to surprise your customer with unexpected service than to disappoint them by promising something you can't guarantee. For instance, Sales Rep A tells his customer, "No problem. I can have those goods delivered in a day." Sales Rep B says, "The best I can do is have those goods delivered in three days." The goods are delivered in two days. Who looks better? Sales Rep B, because he exceeded the customer's expectation and delivered the goods a day early. It's possible that being honest and saying you can't deliver in one day will cost you some business. But suppose they're counting on your delivery, and you can't follow through? You've lost a customer for life.

✓ **Become a "partner" in your customer's business.** Keep your customer's best interests in mind. In very rare cases—if you know that you don't have the right product in your line, or if you know that someone else can make a faster delivery—you might even recommend your competition. If you do that, you'll no longer be considered a salesperson by your customer— you'll be a consultant, a partner. That's integrity selling, and that's the first thing customers talk about when asked what they want in a vendor. The next time you recommend one of your products to this customer, he'll trust that your recommendation is in his best interest.

Five tips to keep customers coming back

1. Maintain a positive attitude and generate enthusiasm.

2. Differentiate yourself through personal touches and exceptional service.

3. Know your customer's business.

4. Make follow-up and feedback high priorities.

5. Give customers reasons—and incentives—to refer you to others.

How to get your customers to sell for you

The best way to get prospective clients to buy from you is to introduce them to other satisfied customers. It's one thing to tell a potential customer how great your product is and how wonderful your follow-up will be, but it's quite another to get him to believe you. Some unscrupulous salespeople will say anything to make a sale. How can you prove that you are sincere and trustworthy? By letting your customers do the talking for you.

There are dozens of ways to build a customer reference sales portfolio, and here are a few:

✓ **Taped testimonials.** Ask your best customers if you can "interview" them on tape about the positive experiences they've had with your product and company. It will only take a few minutes, as you want to put several short interviews on a tape. When you start the interview, introduce yourself and the person you're interviewing. Mention the particular product or service this client is using. Have the customer tell about the reasons he chose to go with your company, and how your product has fulfilled his needs. Then, when a prospect wants to know about your service record, you can say, "Here are some comments from customers who had the same concerns as you do." You can play the tape for him right then, or leave it with him to listen at his leisure.

✓ **Reference letters.** Most sales reps use reference letters, but not enough of them. You should have a reference letter for each account that was interviewed on the tape, so the letter confirms the validity of the taped interviews. Highlight key points. Reference letters don't just arrive spontaneously. Call your customers and ask if they are satisfied with your product and service. Take some notes, get a copy of their letterhead, type up their comments, and bring it in for them to sign. The beauty of this process is that as you're collecting letters, you're building a better relationship with your customers. Of course, the best reference letters are the ones that come to you unsolicited.

✓ **Use a "story" reference list.** When potential customers ask for references, they're usually given a typed list of names and phone numbers. They may or may not call the people on the list, and if they do, they'll probably call one or two and ignore the rest. Why not turn this reference list into a selling tool? Expand your list to include not only names and phone numbers, but mini-stories describing how your product or service has worked for your customers. Write short profiles of their businesses, including which of your products they use and problems you helped solve. Write brief stories of why they bought from you, who they looked at besides you, and why the decision was made. This gives the prospect some insight into which of your customers are similar to him, and makes your references stand out from your competitors'.

✓ **Put your customers in the picture.** If your product is highly technical or complex, you might want to make a videotape of an installation (with the customer's permission, of course). Ask your customers to talk about the benefits they've received from your product or service. If your product is not as complex, take photographs of your customers using your product or service. A picture of a happy, satisfied customer is worth a thousand impersonal sales brochures.

✓ **Ask for mini business card testimonials.** When you make a sale, ask your customer for a business card. Then ask her to jot down on the back of the card one or two main reasons she bought from you. Slip collected cards into a sheet of plastic sleeves you can buy at any office supply store. This is a convenient way to show prospects a variety of your present customers and their handwritten testimonials.

✓ **Use your reference portfolio to answer objections.** For example, if a prospect says, "Your price is too high; I can get it for $2,000 less," you can answer with the reference portfolio: "Many of our present customers said the same thing before they bought from us, but here's what they're saying now after making that extra investment." By using the customer reference portfolio, you can show prospects your successful relationships with present customers. That's an extremely powerful selling tool.

Get your customers to sell for you checklist

✓ **Remember that word of mouth is the most powerful sales tool.** If you do your best for your customers, they'll let others know. Every customer should be treated as if she were the biggest account you have. You never know who may recommend you to whom, and you want to be sure that every customer is getting 100 percent from you.

✓ **Develop a customer portfolio.** Put all your letters of reference, your customer photographs, your customer satisfaction surveys and any other relevant material into an attractive presentation book that can be shown to your prospects.

✓ **Thank your customers for their testimonials.** If your customers write you testimonial letters, or agree to be audio- or video-taped, send them a letter of thanks and perhaps even a small gift. This lets them know you appreciate the vote of confidence.

If you have 100 delighted customers, you have 101 people selling your product.

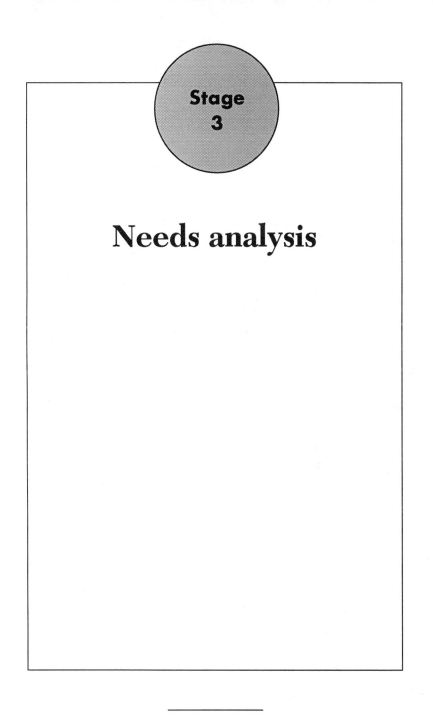

**Stage
3**

Needs analysis

If you were selling shoes, you wouldn't just grab any old pair of shoes regardless of the size, style or color preference of the customer. It would be a miracle if you ever made a match. And yet, many salespeople try to "pitch" prospects into buying before they know anything about them.

New salespeople often feel that the way to keep control of a sale is to keep talking—to go through their presentation point by point, hoping that by the time they're finished they'll have covered the customer's interest. This could not be further from the truth. A presentation can only be effective if you know what the customer's interest is beforehand, and purposely hit each point.

That's where needs analysis comes in. Once you know the customer's needs, you can determine how your product or service can best meet those needs. There are three ways to do this:

1. Research.
2. Asking questions.
3. Listening.

The more information you can gather, the better the solutions you have to offer and the more you elevate yourself above your competitors.

Research

The amount of research you do before you go on sales calls often depends on how many calls you have to make and how much time you have to make them. Obviously, if you're making 20 calls in one day, your research time will be fairly limited. However, time spent in preliminary research will save you time during the sales call. You can make lasting impressions on prospective customers by understanding their business, their industry and their needs. Any information you can find out before a meeting helps you develop the right questions and positions you as a knowledgeable potential "partner" in their business.

If possible, before you go on the sales call find out about:

- The company's origin.
- The company's position within the industry.
- The company's products or services.
- The company's mission statement.
- The company's customers.
- The company's main competitors.

There are many resources from which to do this type of research. They include:

✓ **The library.** If it's a large company, look up the listing in Dun & Bradstreet, and use the library's computer to see if there have been any articles about it in national newspapers or magazines. If it's a smaller company, find out if the local papers have printed any news concerning the company in the past year or so. If your customer's company is a subsidiary, find out about the parent company as well. If you can't find information on the company itself, look for information about the industry as a whole.

✓ **Written information.** Call the company and ask to see any literature it has available, such as brochures, catalogs, newsletters and annual reports. Try to get on the company's mailing list so that you'll have updated information whenever you call.

✓ **Oral information.** Call the customer service department and get as much information from them as you can. Use your networking skills; see if you can find someone who knows a person that works for your prospect company. Talk to salespeople from related industries, and see what they can tell you. If possible, talk to your customer's customers, and find out what they like about this company and what problems, if any, they have with them.

Develop a list of five questions that you would like to have answered before you call on your next prospect. Then do the research necessary to answer those questions.

Research checklist

Keep, and update, a list of reference sources. Some of those might include:

✓ **Annual reports/SEC Filings.** You might even want to buy a share of stock in the company. That way you'll be on the mailing list for all corporate financial information. Read the annual report's letter from the top executive and the mission statement. Read all of the footnotes, because they often mention potential problems. And look for the list of officers and top executives.

✓ **Dun & Bradstreet, Value Line, U.S. Industrial Outlook.** These sources provide information on companies and industries, including trends and major players.

✓ **Trade Association Directory.** Look up the association appropriate to your prospect. Then call that association; they can give you industry information and tell you which industry publications would be appropriate for you to read.

✓ **Trade publications.** When you find publications relevant to your prospect's industry, use them to give you information about your prospect's competitors as well. Don't forget to check out the advertising (which can be as informative as the articles), new product information, and sections about who's been hired and/or promoted.

✓ **Directories and Who's Who.** Ask your librarian for appropriate national, regional and/or local business directories. They'll often provide detailed information about companies and their chief executives.

✓ **Chamber of Commerce Directories.** Call the Chamber of Commerce for your territory and ask for a directory. This will usually provide a listing of businesses as well as basic facts about what they do, the number of people they employ and names of key executives.

The art of asking questions

Selling is not a one-size-fits-all process. Every prospect's needs, challenges, problems, budget and decision-making process is unique. Therefore, every sale must be designed and customized to fit that prospect's needs.

There is only one way to find out what those needs are, and that is by asking questions. Questions are a salesperson's most valuable selling tool. Every salesperson knows that in order to sell a product or service, you have to sell its benefits. But what's a benefit to one person may be of no interest to another. The only way to find out which benefits are important to a particular prospect is to ask questions.

Most prospects expect you to come in and make a pitch about your product or service. However, you can surprise and impress them by getting information from them first. You can start your presentation with:

"Thanks for sharing this time with me today, Mr. Smith. As you know, we are an advertising specialty company with 25 years in the business. We've been working with many businesses in this area. But before I begin to tell you in more detail about our organization and what we do, I'd like to find out as much as I can about your company, your people and your goals, so that I can see if we have an opportunity to make a match here. Do you mind if I ask you some questions and take some notes?"

Key qualifying questions

Here are some key questions that will allow your prospect to share important information. Customize these questions to your own industry and use those that work best for you. The more you know about your customers needs, the better you can recommend the right product or service and the greater the odds are for closing the business.

- What are the three most important criteria you consider when investing in _____ (fill in the name of your product or service)?
- I know your main area is _____, but can you tell me more about your company's products and its history?
- What differentiates you from your competition?
- Who are your main customers? What do they expect from your product or service?
- What is your role in the organization?
- What are your company goals for the next one, two or three years?
- How can I become your most valued supplier?
- What does the next vendor/supplier need to do to earn your business?
- What would have to happen for you to consider a switch from your present vendor/supplier?
- What would you like to see from a vendor and salesperson in the area of support after the sale?
- What is the process you normally go through when considering a new vendor?
- Who else would be involved in this decision that you would recommend speaking with?
- What are the reasons you've changed to your present vendor from the one you had in the past?
- How many suppliers do you currently use?
- Do you have a system for evaluating the service and results of your suppliers?
- What is the biggest challenge in your business?
- What do you like most about your job?

- What services provided by your present supplier are most important to you? To your company? To your customer?

- What do you like least about your job?

- What is it about this business you don't like?

- What are your feelings about our industry?

- If we could develop an agreement that added value to your program in both price and service, would it be of interest to you?

- Do you see any reason why you would not want to utilize our company?

Of course, you don't have to ask all of these questions all of the time. Be sure that you understand why you're asking a particular question, so you know what to listen for in the answer. For instance, the answer to "What is the process you normally go through when considering a new vendor?" will tell you the exact steps this customer uses to acquire new vendors. The answer to "What are your feelings about our industry?" will tell you if they've had problems with companies like yours in the past. If they have, you can address those problems and assure the prospect that you can deal with those issues should they arise. The answer to "What are the reasons you've changed to your present vendor from the one you had in the past?" will show you buying patterns, how the company has grown and how they make a decision to change.

The four basic types of questions

1. General questions. General questions gather basic information about the company, its departments, its customers, its competition and the individual with whom you're speaking. These are usually open-ended questions, such as "What got you into this business?" (General questions are similar to those that might be asked by a psychiatrist to get the patient to open up: "Can you tell me what you've gone through these past three years?")

2. Probing questions. Once we find the general information, we want to get more specific. These questions uncover problems, concerns, dissatisfactions or specific buying criteria. The key is to probe beneath the surface and get information the competition misses. These questions can be either open or closed: "You said earlier you just opened a new branch office. What type of system are they using there?" Every time you ask a general question, you'll probably want to follow up with some probing questions that will help you get the specific information you need. These are questions like: "Can you expand on that for me?" "Can you tell me more about that?" "Can you describe exactly how that works?" (These are like questions a reporter might ask: "Where was the fire?" "When did it happen?" "Who did you see?")

3. Effect questions. These questions enable the prospect to express the impact of daily problems and how they affect their business, customers and employees. The purpose is to get problems out in the open so that you can show how your product or service can effect a solution. You might ask, "Are there any problems with the new system? How does that affect your delivery schedule?" (These are they type of questions a doctor might ask: "What happens when these headaches come on?" "Do they affect your eyesight? Your balance? Your mobility?")

4. Commitment questions. These questions prompt the prospect to express a clear desire for a solution. They take the focus away from the problem and towards the value of a solution. *The prospect herself* expresses the worth and value of what a solution would mean to her: "So having a product that could eliminate those problems would be important to you?" You're helping the prospect to see how your product or service would fill a need for her, and you're getting "yeses" throughout the sales cycle, so the close is a natural progression. (Lawyers ask commitment questions: "So what you're saying is that on Tuesday, November 4, you were at the meeting with Mr. Jones, isn't that right?")

You don't have to ask questions in any specific order. Start with very broad questions and then go into specifics. Use open-ended questions to get information, and closed-ended questions to gain commitment.

> *People don't care how much you know*
> *until they know how much you care.*

Questioning checklist

✓ **Take notes.** Don't rely on your memory to remind you of what's important to your prospect. Ask up front if it's all right for you to take notes. Write down key points and hot buttons you can refer to later in your presentation.

✓ **Develop your own list of "best" questions.** Keep a "key qualifying questions" sheet, like the one on page 59, for each of your customers, filling in the 10 most important qualifying questions you should ask.

Key qualifying questions

COMPANY INFORMATION

Date: _____

Account: _____

Phone: _____

Address:

_____

_____

_____

Contact Name: _____ **Title:** _____

Number of locations, divisions, affiliates and subsidiaries: _____
(May we please have a list with names and addresses of each?)

1. _____
2. _____
3. _____
4. _____
5. _____
6. _____
7. _____
8. _____
9. _____
10. _____

Ask if you can take a tour of the customer's business. This accomplishes two things:

1. It gives you an insider's view. If you're selling computers, for instance, you may be able to see for yourself what system the customer currently owns and how it's actually used.

2. It gives the customer recognition and a chance to show off what she does and what she's done with her company. It's a great opportunity to build rapport and let your customers know that you're interested and that you care.

The art of listening

There are three key elements in real estate, and they are location, location, location. The three key elements in sales are listening, listening, listening. Listening enables you to understand each prospect and customize your presentation to focus on this prospect's needs. There have been many times that sales reps have talked themselves out of a sale, but none have ever listened themselves out of a sale.

If you're talking, you're not learning anything. When your prospects are talking, they're revealing clues about themselves and their business. If you're a good listener, you can pick up on these clues and focus your presentation on these areas. If you let the buyer tell you what her needs are, it cuts your work in half.

✓ **Watch body language.** If a customer is leaning forward, making eye contact with you and using animated gestures, he or she is hitting on a particular area of interest. If the customer is leaning back, distracted and slumping in her seat, her body language is telling you to move on to another area. Learn to listen with your eyes as well as your ears.

✓ **Show interest and alertness.** Your body language also conveys signals to the prospect. Be an active listener. If the prospect thinks you're not interested, she'll end the conversation. Make frequent eye contact. Take notes. Sit up straight and nod your head to let her know you're following what's being said.

✓ **Eliminate distractions.** You may not be able to eliminate the distractions in someone else's office, but you can eliminate your own distractions.

✓ **Delay interpretation.** Don't jump to conclusions, and don't interrupt. Wait until the prospect is through speaking. Listen for hot buttons, but don't jump to the close too quickly. There'll be plenty of time to close when the prospect has finished her thought.

✓ **Put aside personal opinions.** You may not like a prospect's opinions or political views. Your only job is to find out whether or not your product or service can help that prospect's business.

✓ **Don't judge a book by its cover.** The head of a company isn't always dressed in a conservative suit. Don't decide from the speaker's appearance and delivery that what he or she has to say is not worthwhile.

✓ **Avoid expectations.** There will be times when your products and the customer's need simply do not match. If that's the case, move on to another sale. Don't try to force this customer into a mold that doesn't fit. But be sure to ask if this prospect knows anyone else who might benefit from your product or service.

✓ **Check your understanding.** Your interpretation of what the prospect said may be something different than what he or she actually meant. "Our computer system is adequate for our present needs," may be taken to mean no interest in a new system. To clarify, you might ask, "Does that mean you're completely satisfied with your present system?" That gives the prospect the opportunity to say, "Not really. It's adequate for the present, but it doesn't leave much room for future expansion." By making sure you understand the answer, you exposed a need and created an opportunity for further discussion.

✓ **Listen between the lines.** Often what a person *doesn't* say provides as much information as what she does say.

Follow-up

If you have a short sales cycle, you may be able to close the sale after you complete your presentation. In a longer sales cycle, the needs analysis is only the beginning of your relationship with this prospect. You may be asked to forward information or materials to the prospect, see this prospect again, or make an appointment to see someone else in the company.

Whatever the outcome of your meeting, be sure to follow up with a letter summarizing the main points of your discussion. Go over the prospect's needs and desires. This shows that you were listening. Also include a statement that tells the prospect the next action you will be taking, such as calling on a particular date or coming in for the next appointment.

Here's a typical letter that is sent to prospects after a needs analysis meeting:

Ms. Sally Trainer, V.P., Sales and Marketing
Acme Button Company
1 Main Street
Anytown, USA 10000

Dear Sally:

It was a pleasure speaking with you this afternoon. I'm very impressed with your recent award for sales manager of the year. Thanks again for taking the time to share your valuable input. Enclosed is the information I promised you. To make sure that we're on the right track, the following list is to review some of the key points you brought up:

- You need a system that handles a large volume of calls.
- Callers should have the option of voice-mail or operator-answered calls.
- All staff, including President and CEO, must be trained on the system.
- Follow-up plan must be written out in detail.

As we discussed, I'll be calling you on Friday, September 30, at 9 a.m. to go over this information along with any questions you may have. If you need anything before then, please feel free to call. As a representative of XYZ Corporation, I look forward to starting a long and successful relationship with you and your organization.

Best regards,

John J. Doe

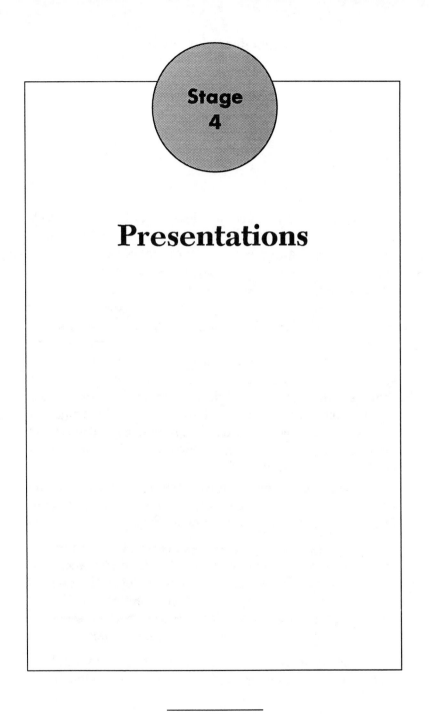

**Stage
4**

Presentations

Imagine you're a customer looking to buy a new widget. Two salespeople come along with essentially the same product, pricing and promises. What makes you choose one over the other? More than likely, the salesperson you chose had a powerful, persuasive presentation.

Presentations come in many forms, shapes and sizes. Actually, any sales call you make is a form of presentation. Some calls, however, include more formal presentations with visual aids, leave-behinds and product demonstrations. You can shape your presentation around a portfolio that contains information you go through in an organized manner, or you can select only those pieces of information that have an impact on a particular customer. The type of presentation you give depends on your product, your prospect and your personal style.

A mediocre presentation can lose the sale for even the greatest product or service. Keeping that in mind, here are five things *not* to do when making a presentation:

- ✓ **Speak more than 80 percent of the time.** The most successful reps *listen* 70 to 80 percent of the time and make an effort to learn the real needs of the buyer. Once you understand the customer's criteria, you can customize the presentation to show how you can meet their needs.

- ✓ **Wing it.** Don't go into your meeting blind. Find out as much as possible about the customer before you go into the call. Customers respect the salesperson who takes a genuine interest in their situation and makes the effort to understand their business ahead of time.

✓ **Don't take any notes.** A short pencil is better than a long memory. Ask the customer if it's okay to take notes because you don't want to miss any information.

✓ **Just start rambling about your product and go off on tangents.** How can you expect your prospect to follow your lead if you don't know where you're going? A presentation must have a clear, logical through-line so that the sale is always moving forward and the prospect is always heading toward the ultimate "yes."

✓ **Don't ask any questions.** The question is the answer. The most successful reps in the country ask powerful questions to get their customers talking about their real needs. That's the only way to be able to focus your presentation on the buyer's criteria.

The purpose of your presentation is to make it easy for the customer to buy.

Six steps to a powerful presentation

Every time you make a sales call, your presentation will be different than it was the time before. That's not only because each prospect you encounter will have different needs; other factors come into play, including the time the prospect has available to spend with you and the prospect's personality type.

However, the basic structure of your presentation need never change and will serve as the solid foundation on which you build your sales. That foundation is based on the following six steps:

- ✓ **Visualize a successful outcome.** Right before you make the call, run through the entire process in your mind. Go over the steps you're going to take and the points you need to make. Read over your research notes and the ways you've found that your product can benefit this customer. Picture yourself coming up with new benefits as you learn more about the company's needs.

- ✓ **Introduction/building rapport.** Try to find areas of mutual interest you can chat about briefly. Your research might have told you the prospect went to the same college you did, or that the company is opening a branch in your home town. Look around the office. Find an area of common ground to give the conversation a smoother start.

- ✓ **Bridge to the business topic.** There should be no awkward pause or jump from the short introductory period into the business at hand. You must take the lead and set the direction for your presentation. The leadership you show when you're clearly in control adds to your persuasiveness as a presenter.

  Here is a typical bridging transition, which you would, of course, customize for your own business:

  "Mr. Jones, I appreciate you sharing your time with me today. As you probably know, my company, Widgets, Inc., has been the leader in manufacturing widgets since 1956. We've worked with many companies in this area, including ABC Company and XYZ Corporation. But before I go into the specifics about our widgets, I'd like to find out information about your needs, your goals and what you're looking for in a widget supplier. At that point I'll be able to see if we can help you the way we've helped our other customers. Do you mind if I ask you some questions and take some notes?"

✓ **Questions/needs analysis.** This is the stage where you use the questioning techniques discussed in the last section. That means most of this time will be spent listening and taking notes.

✓ **Summarize.** Here's where you do the talking—although even in this stage, you're constantly asking for the customer's feedback. Go back through your notes and summarize the customer's key buying criteria. For instance, you might say, "So the most important point for you when buying widgets is that they be available for immediate delivery on short notice. Is that right? You also said that you need to be able to special-order widgets in non-standard sizes. That's also important to you, isn't it?"

There are three reasons for summarizing the key points:

1. It allows you to make sure you're communicating well. You may have interpreted something incorrectly. This way, you give the prospect an opportunity to say, "What I really meant was..."

2. It shows you really have been listening and taking notes, and that you care about what's important to the customer.

3. It enables you to judge whether or not you actually have a match. If you have a good match, you can then continue with your presentation, customizing it to emphasize the benefits that fit this prospect's needs.

✓ **Close for the next step.** In a few instances, you may decide that there is no match or opportunity there. In most cases, you'll want to close for the next step, whether that is more research ("Is there someone I can speak to in the shipping department so that I can get a better feel for your needs in that area?"); setting up a demonstration ("I've got a good feeling about this. I'd like to show you exactly how the product will meet your needs. Which would be a better time for you, Tuesday morning or Wednesday afternoon?"); or closing for the business ("Why don't we go ahead with this today?").

A powerful presentation is always interactive. Questions you should be asking throughout: "Are we on track?" "Is this clear to you?" "Is this something that's important to you?"

Powerful presentations checklist

1. Visualize a successful outcome.

2. Introduction/building rapport.

3. Bridge to the business topic.

4. Questions/needs analysis.

5. Summarize.

6. Close for the next step.

✓ **Be yourself.** There is no one secret to success; there are many factors that go into peak achievement. But there is one secret to failure—and that's trying to be liked by everyone. Don't try to be the perfect salesperson. Do what makes you feel comfortable, and your customers will be comfortable with you.

✓ **Preparation is the key.** The greatest fear we all have is to go into a situation unprepared (like a surprise exam in a class you haven't attended all year). Preparation and practice are the best possible antidotes for fear and lack of confidence. Here are four steps that will help you prepare for any sales call:

✓ **Think about your objective.** Be sure you have a clearly stated purpose for each call.

✓ **Do your research.** Learn as much you can about each prospective customer.

✓ **Prepare all visual aids and support materials**. Be sure you have all necessary forms, contracts, brochures, demonstration aids, customer portfolio materials, etc.

✓ **Review your benefit statements and customer testimonials**. Remind yourself of what is best about your product and about you as a salesperson.

The four t's of presentation

Even though no two presentations you give will be the same—they'll be customized to emphasize the benefits for the individual prospect—there is a pattern you can follow to guarantee a successful presentation. That pattern is described by the four T's of presentations:

✓ **Tell them what you're going to tell them.** Prospects will follow you much more willingly if they sense you know where you're going and how you're going to get there. So you might open your presentation with a statement like, "What I'm going to do is take you through our new product line and demonstrate exactly how we can help you decrease production time." Now you've got them hooked and waiting to hear the information you've got.

✓ **Tell them.** Go through your presentation following the outline you proposed above. Be brief, but passionate. Your prospect will know if you don't believe in what you're saying. Keep your thoughts clear and succinct and present your ideas in a logical sequence.

✓ **Test them.** Powerful presentations are interactive. You want to keep the customer involved. "Based on what you said earlier, time frame is important to you. Using our widget, we can have you automated and on-line within two weeks. Would that be helpful in meeting your time frame?" If the prospect says "yes," you can follow with, "How else do you see yourself benefiting from that?" Ask questions that will get you feedback. You want to know if the presentation is hitting home, making sense and addressing their criteria.

✓ **Tell them what you told them.** Summarize your ideas so that the presentation is focused. "What we just looked at was the new product line from Widgets, Inc. and the four key ways these products can help grow your business. Did you see how this can be of great benefit to your company?"

Testing is the most important of the four T's. It will keep you on track, keep you focused on the customer's needs and keep the sale moving forward toward the close.

Four t's checklist

✓ Tell them what you're going to tell them.
✓ Tell them.
✓ Test them.
✓ Tell them what you told them.

Customizing presentations for your customer's needs

The number one sales strategy for the '90s is customer service. This philosophy applies even before the customer is officially yours. It's your job to let the customer know you're there to service his needs.

Even a mediocre presentation can result in a sale if it's focused on why this particular customer should buy this particular product. Here are some important ideas to keep in mind for customizing your presentations:

- ✓ **Complete a thorough needs analysis.** Write down a list of key questions before you go into the call. Be sure to probe and clarify until you get the information you need. Then refer to your notes frequently so that you're always speaking to your product's benefits as they relate to the prospect's needs.

- ✓ **Present your ideas from the prospect's perspective.** People buy for their reasons, not yours. If you speak to their real needs, they'll be compelled to listen and listen well. What does your prospect care about? Figure that out and you're well on your way to the sale.

- ✓ **Make the connections between product and benefit clear.** Don't assume that because it's obvious to you, it's clear to the prospect as well. Say something like, "Our new line of notebook computers weighs 40 percent less than the old line, which makes them easily portable. You mentioned that light weight and portability were important factors in your decision, isn't that right?"

- ✓ **Use layman's terms.** You might think that fancy names and gadgetry are impressive, but they're not if the prospect doesn't know what you're talking about. Start talking about "duplexing mode" or "horizontal frequency" and you'll lose the person—even though these features may benefit the customer. Don't bury the benefits in

technical jargon. Linking the product and benefit usually results in clarity and persuasion.

Always remember that the customer is asking:
"What's in it for me?" "How do I benefit?" "So what?"

Customizing presentations checklist

✓ **Prioritize your prospect's needs,** and address the most important issues first.

✓ **Learn to be empathetic.** When you're tuned-
in to a prospect or customer, you understand
what the prospect is trying to say and what he
really means. You're even able to understand
needs the prospect might not fully recognize. It
is empathy—the ability to understand what
others are feeling—that gives a successful
salesperson the competitive edge.

Presentations with pizzazz

You don't have to be an entertainer or magician, or fill
your presentations with bells, whistles and special effects.
But you do want to make it interesting and get your prospect as excited about your product as you are. You want
your presentations to be vivid, convincing and memorable.
Here are some suggestions to help you achieve that goal:

✓ **Be enthusiastic.** Enthusiasm is the outward
manifestation of our inner passion. It is a force
that lifts our spirits, gives us confidence and

makes us feel empowered. It gives us energy. Enthusiasm can carry us far beyond any skill or talent we may be lacking. In many instances, we can override our deficiencies by turning on an engine of enthusiasm. And enthusiasm is catching. If you're excited and passionate about what you're selling, your prospect will have a strong desire to share that passion with you.

✓ **Don't overload your audience.** Because you're passionate and enthusiastic, you may be tempted to share everything you know about your product or service. The truth is, your prospects only need to know what's relevant to them. People won't retain an overload of information. They can read the facts in your brochures and sales materials—your job is to make the information interesting. Too many facts, and people's minds begin to wander. According to some studies, the average attention span is eight seconds. So you're better off concentrating on the three or four points most important to your prospect.

✓ **Use stories to illustrate your points.** In order to demonstrate exactly how your product can fill this prospect's needs, talk about how other customers with similar needs were able to solve their problems by using your product or service. Show how you worked with that customer to find the solution and how you can do the same for this prospect. If you have a written or taped testimonial from this satisfied customer, use this opportunity to present it to your prospect.

✓ **Make eye contact.** Your eyes are your most important physical feature as a salesperson, because they are crucial in establishing rapport. Your eyes are your first direct contact with your prospect—they should be conveying the message that you're glad to be here. Don't stare at your prospect; that will only make him uncomfortable. On the other hand, don't stare at your notes or your sales materials the whole time. Continue to make periodic eye contact throughout the presentation.

✓ **Use vivid language.** The way you say something often has more impact than what you're actually saying. You can increase the power and persuasiveness of your presentations by making some simple changes in the way that you speak. Using voice inflection and enthusiasm in your presentation makes a greater impact on your message.

✓ **Use your voice as a sales tool.** When you're telemarketing, your voice is responsible for the entire impression you make on your listener. In person, other factors come into play, but your voice still says a lot about you. Be aware of various aspects of your voice:

- Speak at a moderate rate. Don't speak too fast or too slow.

- Be aware of your volume. Speak too softly and no one will hear you; shout and people will be offended.

- Enunciate. Don't mumble or slur your words.

• Take voice, speech or public speaking classes to improve the quality of your voice.

Practice makes perfect. Grab your friends and family and role-play presentations with them.

Presentations with pizzazz checklist

✓ **Say what you mean as simply as possible.** Big words don't necessarily make you sound knowledgeable. They can make you sound phony. Be yourself. Use the type of language you normally use.

✓ **Eliminate bad language habits.** People often fall into habits of speech that weaken their message. Eliminate phrases like "perhaps," "I think," "maybe," "I believe," "you know," "sort of" and "kind of." If you have a strong opinion, state it. "This is the most cost-effective solution" is a much stronger statement than, "I think this is a pretty good cost-effective solution."

✓ **Use descriptive language.** Draw mental pictures for your listener. You want your prospects to be able to imagine themselves using your product, so use phrases that include them. You might say, "When you use our product, you will..." or "We can have these widgets delivered to your factory door in three days."

Six-step demonstration

Some products require demonstrations that may take place a few days or a few weeks after the initial presentation. Here are the six steps to successful demonstrations:

1. **Introduction/summary of buying criteria.** Start off by saying, "Before I begin the demonstration, I want you to know I'm going to be concentrating on these three benefits, which you said were most important to you. Then I'll go over some other benefits and answer any questions."

2. **Ask if anything has changed.** You want to find out if there are any changes or additions to the buying criteria since you last spoke, so that, if necessary, you can add them to your demonstration.

3. **Precommitment.** You don't want to be too pushy, but you do want to say something like, "If you can see how this will benefit your organization, do we have a basis for going ahead with this today?" If this doesn't gain commitment, it will get any objections or questions out into the open.

4. **Demonstrate: Feature-Function-Benefit.** You control the demonstration. Show the feature, explain what it does, and show how it will assist with the prospect's key needs.

5. **Summarize demonstration criteria.** Tell them what you told them. Here's where you review the key benefits of the product, based on the customer's needs. That way, you make sure the customer sees how your product will be of value to him.

6. **Close for the next step.** Make sure you've etiher set a time for an additional appointment or demonstration, or even closed the sale at this point. Sometimes if you're not sure where to go, there's nothing wrong with asking the customer his input ("John, what would be your recommendation for our next step?"). Or if you have earned the right to close for the business, just simply say "John, let's go ahead with this. The close should be natural and nonmanipulative. This step is covered in Stage 6, beginning on page 89.

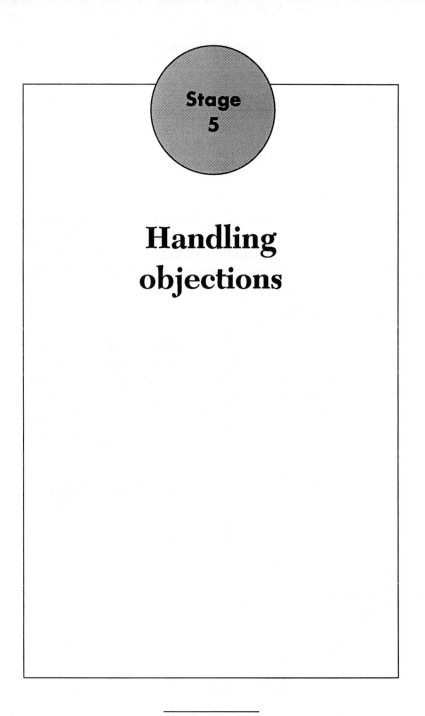

Stage 5

Handling objections

If it weren't for objections, there would be no salespeople. There would only be order takers. Although objections are often seen as barriers to sales, they're really road signs; they show you the way to proceed with the sale. They let you know the prospect's concerns and allow you to demonstrate how your product or service can alleviate those concerns and fill the prospect's needs.

Beginning salespeople often *create* objections by trying to close before they have qualified the prospect or established the value of their product. You can't eliminate all objections. However, if you become proficient in the three preceding selling stages (prospecting, needs analysis and presentation), you'll be able to answer objections before they come up.

Objections are not obstacles, they're opportunities to provide solutions and move on to the next step of the sale.

Five-step method to handling customer concerns

1. Listen.
2. Question.
3. Rephrase/convert.
4. Present solution.
5. Close for the next step.

1. **Listen to the entire objection.** Too many times, salespeople, who have heard objections from many different prospects, jump in before the prospect they're working with has finished speaking. This causes the prospect to think you're not listening to him. Another mistake salespeople make is that they take objections personally and get defensive. The prime reason salespeople lose business is due to lack of communication with their customers.

   Pause for a few seconds when a prospect raises an objection. Let him know you've taken his comment seriously, and that you're not going to give him an answer you've used on dozens of other customers.

2. **Question.** The best way to answer objections is often with a question. You want to find out what, specifically, the prospect is objecting to. Suppose a prospect says, "I'm not sure about going with your company. I've heard some negative things about your service." You might be tempted to say, "First of all, I don't know if you know this but last year we won a national award for the best service department in the country..." This is a defensive answer and doesn't calm the customer's concerns.

   Instead, ask, "What kind of 'negative things' have you heard?" Then, when the customer says, "I understand that service operators put people on hold for half an hour, or else say they'll call back and do so two days later. I can't afford to wait that long for service." That gives you an opportunity to tell the prospect the company has added 20 new service operators and play a taped testimonial from a customer who had been experiencing service problems, but is now pleased with the improved service department.

---

3. **Rephrase/convert.** When you rephrase, you have an opportunity to change a general concern into a specific problem, which you can then address. Convert the objection into a question. "So having an efficient and timely service department is important to you?" The customer has to agree with you, because it's a problem he brought up. When you rephrase and convert, it shows the prospect you're listening and understanding what he's saying.

You can start your paraphrase with key lead-ins that will help clarify the objections, such as:

- "If I understand you correctly, your concern is..."
- "What I hear you saying is..."
- "So what you mean is..."

End your paraphrase with a closed-ended question that gains agreement, such as:

- "Isn't that right?"
- "Is that what you mean?"
- "Does that answer your question?"

4. **Present the solution.** Once the customer feels you understand the problem, you can demonstrate how your product or service will fill his needs.

5. **Close for the next step.** This step is covered in Stage 6, beginning on page 89.

Dealing with tough customers

Every salesperson runs into tough customers once in a while. When you do, you may want to simply give up and go home. But if you know what to look for, and how the four basic types of tough customers like to be handled, you can turn a tough customer into a long-term buyer. Here are some suggestions for handling the "tough" ones:

- ✓ **The Talker.** What started out as a meeting that should have taken 15 minutes is turning into a two-hour marathon because the customer keeps talking. You don't want to be rude, and it looks like he might buy, but... Some people just like to talk. Unfortunately, you don't have the time (and neither do they, really) to spend chatting. Give the talker a chance to get out what he wants to say. Listen, wait for a pause, then asked a closed-ended question that will direct him back to the subject at hand.

- ✓ **The Complainer.** Complainers want more from you than just solving their problems. They want someone to listen to them, and take their complaints seriously. Be empathetic. Say, "I understand what you mean," or "That must have been difficult for you." Take notes, write down their complaints, and tell them what actions you plan to take. You might say, "I'll get that information and fax it to you tomorrow," or "I understand that you've had trouble reaching me when I'm on the road. Why don't I give you my beeper number? That way, I can get back to you within 5 minutes, no matter where I am."

- ✓ **The Know-It-All.** The know-it-all comes across as the toughest type to handle, but is really the easiest—once you know how. This person needs to feel important. He's the kind who will say, "I've been in business for 40 years. You can't tell me anything I don't already know." The best way to handle this personality is to acknowledge, and show your appreciation for, his experience and expertise. You might say, "I didn't know you'd been in the business that long. You must know an awful lot about this industry. How did you get started?"

Show a genuine interest in them and their business. Be sincere. These people can spot a phony a mile away. But they like to be mentors to people who are genuinely interested in what they have to say, and they can be extremely loyal customers if you treat them with the respect they really do deserve.

✓ **The Quiet One.** With this personality type, you'll get the best results if you rely on the power of questions. Questions can get even the shyest, most reserved of people to open up. If you're finding it difficult to get the information you need, use open-ended questions that get the prospect more involved. Begin these questions with phrases like:

- "What do you mean by..."
- "Describe to me..."
- "Can you go into more detail about..."
- "Can you explain that further..."

Handling objections checklist

✓ **Don't argue.** Once you start arguing, you've lost. You're trying to help your prospect solve his problem; you're not trying to persuade him to do something he doesn't want to do. You're not out to prove the prospect wrong or make him feel stupid for voicing his concern. When the prospect objects, he's really saying, "I need more information on this point (i.e., price, service, benefits) before I can go on with the sale."

✓ **Let your present customers help you handle prospects' objections.** Use the "feel, felt, found" process described on page 32. Say, "I understand how you feel. A lot of my present customers felt the same way you do. But when they found the exceptional value they got for their money, they made the decision to buy from us. By the way, here are three of my customers on tape who can tell what I'm talking about." Then play your taped testimonials for the prospect, and let your customers sell for you.

✓ **Confirm that you've answered an objection completely.** You may think you've answered the prospect's question. There's a chance, however, that you weren't entirely clear or that other questions popped into the prospect's mind. So end your answer with a question: "That answers your concern about service, doesn't it?" "Have I clarified that point for you?" "I think we've found the way to solve that problem, don't you agree?"

The bitterness of poor quality remains long after the sweetness of low price is forgotten.

**Stage
6**

Closing

You won't find "150 ways to close the sale" in this section. In fact, this section is only a few pages long. Successful salespeople don't need fancy closing techniques because they've earned the sale from start to finish.

Everything you do, from the first time you meet the customer and make her feel comfortable with you, to the time she signs on the bottom line, is part of the close. In every sale, both parties are meant to benefit from the transaction—the salesperson by selling the product or service and the customer by finding a way to solve his or her problem.

Customers are more intelligent these days. Fancy closes don't work; the last thing you want to do is be manipulative. Closing is not a single step—it's the progression of the preceding stages of selling. If you say you need training in closing techniques, what you really need is a refresher course in prospecting, qualifying, needs analysis, presentation and handling objections. If you're successful in all those stages, you'll be successful in closing.

From the moment you first meet a customer, you're setting up the opportunity to make the close as effective and easy as "Why don't we go ahead with this?"

Six tips for closing success

1. **Ask the right qualifying questions.** You can't sell your product or service to someone who

doesn't want, need or have the ability to pay for it. If you keep trying to sell to this prospect, you'll inevitably fail, and you may be tempted to blame your failure on a lack of closing technique. Top salespeople find out quickly whether or not opportunity for a sale is likely. If so, they're persistent and come back with new information if they don't make a sale right away. But if there is no opportunity there, they increase their prospecting efforts and move on to the next closing possibility.

2. **Remember that you sell what your customer sells.** Your ultimate goal is to understand what your customer's business is about. Get to know who their customers are, what problems they're having, what their goals are and what they see as their greatest challenges. Only then can you find the ways that your product or service can help them achieve their goals, meet their challenges and grow their business.

3. **Get the customer to identify all the problems that might be solved by your product or service.** As you're presenting or demonstrating the key points that meet the needs of your customer, you might say, "Is this something that would help your organization be more productive?" Or, "Would that help eliminate those problems you're having in the plant?" Or, "Can you see how this would be helpful to you?" You're constantly getting "yeses" from the customer to earn the right to move ahead. Then when you do close, you've established ongoing agreement from the customer that your product or service is something that would be beneficial to her and her company.

4. **Get the customer to identify the value of solving the identified problems.** Instead of pointing out the benefits to the customer, you might ask, "How do you see this benefiting your people?" Get them to explain the benefits to you, and they become the product's strongest advocate.

5. **Get agreement that the proposed solution provides the values identified.** This is a review stage: "Now you can see how our product can actually improve productivity in the plant, isn't that right?"

6. **Ask for the business.** The best close in the world is when the customer says, "Why don't we go ahead with this?" Of course, this doesn't happen often, but if you do your work throughout the previous steps, closing should be natural. The only reason salespeople have problems closing is because they haven't earned the right. They're afraid of rejection; they're afraid of losing the business. Sometimes they haven't done enough prospecting for the month, and they're afraid of getting a "no." Sometimes they're afraid to ask for the business too early. But if you ask the right questions, such as "What do we have to do to earn your business," you'll know the steps you need to take. If you never ask for the business, chances are you'll never get it.

Closing checklist

1. Ask the right qualifying questions.

2. Remember that you sell what your customer sells.

3. Get the customer to identify all the problems that might be solved by your product or service.

4. Get the customer to identify the value of solving the identified problems.

5. Get agreement that the proposed solution provides the values identified.

6. Close for the next step.

**Stage
7**

Follow-up

Surveys show that 68 percent of customers leave a particular vendor because they feel that the salesperson doesn't care about them or their business. The way to let a customer know you care is through this stage of the sales cycle, the follow-up. Follow-up is not only a critical part of keeping a customer, it's also critical in generating future business and in using your customers as a referral source.

Your sale doesn't end when the customer signs the order sheet. In fact, that's when it really begins. Top salespeople provide their customers with extraordinary service and support. They become more than a salesperson; they become their customer's advocate and partner. That's what follow-up really means, and that's what, in this day of product parity, will set you apart from the competition.

Customer service is any company's most effective form of advertising.

The 60-second survey

Print the following survey on the back of a business reply card and send it out to all of your customers. Use the results to determine where you need to improve your follow-up and customer service.

Dear Valued Customer:

    To assist us in determining how we may better serve you, please complete and return this survey.

Your Name: _____

Company Name: _____

Phone: _____ Date: _____

Please respond to the following by checking the appropriate boxes at right.

	Excellent	Good	Fair	Poor
1. Courtesy & helpfulness of receptionist				
2. Response to inquiries				
3. Courtesy, attitude & appearance of staff				
4. Our company's communication with customer				
5. Service of company's sales rep(s)				
6. Overall evaluation				

Did sales rep respond to service call right away?

❑ Yes ❑ No

Would you recommend our product to others?

❑ Yes ❑ No

❑ Please call me to discuss my account.

Comments:

_____

_____

_____

_____

Follow-up checklist

✓ **Write thank-you letters for appointments, demonstrations, orders and referrals.** Just a short, handwritten note can make the difference between a one-time sale and a committed customer. This is an easy task that can be done at home while you're watching TV. Yet not many salespeople take the time to do it. This is a sure-fire way of standing out from the rest of the crowd.

✓ **Call the customer right after the sale to be sure he is satisfied.** Find out if the results were what the customer expected. That way you can often ward off small problems before they become larger than necessary.

✓ **Maintain communications for future considerations.** Keep in touch. Call to let the customer know about any new developments, upgrades or additional products you may have available. Call to find out if the customer has any challenges that need to be met and how you can help. Call just to say hello.

✓ **Establish a schedule for follow-up calls and customer visits.** Ask the customer about his or her expectations of a salesperson after a sale. Find out how often they would like you to call: once a week, once a month, once a quarter? Write call-back dates in your calendar so you won't forget.

✓ **Deliver more than you promise.** This is the most effective follow-up of all. Let your customers know they can count on you to help them solve their problems, even after the sale is made. If you do this, you can rest assured they'll come back to you again for the next purchase.

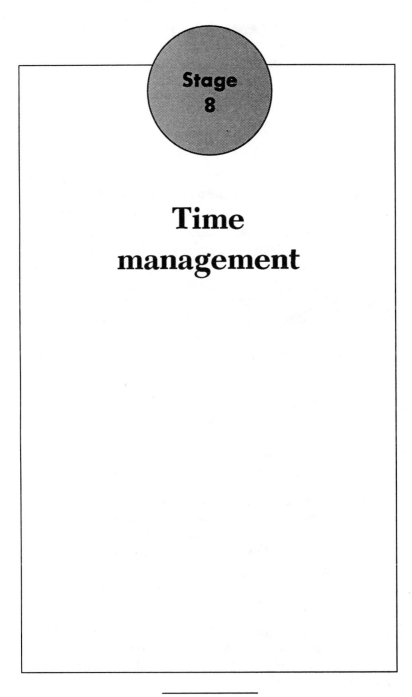

**Stage
8**

Time
management

So many sales calls to make. So much territory to cover. So many letters, proposals, reports to write. So little time.

Sound familiar? Every salesperson faces this same dilemma: how to make the best and most productive use of every working hour. If you constantly feel pressured and worry about what you should be doing next and all that you've yet to accomplish, you can't concentrate on your main goal—generating sales. That's why time management is an absolutely essential skill for sales success. Time management is based on organization, priority and focus. You want to:

- ✓ **Organize** your tasks so that they fall into a logical sequence. This frees up your time so that you're not always running around asking yourself "What should I do next?" You have a plan for the day, the week and/or the month.

- ✓ **Prioritize** your activities so that what *must* get done does get done. Some activities are more urgent than others. List your activities in order of importance; that way if some less important things don't get done, they can be shifted to another day without affecting your sales productivity.

- ✓ **Focus** on the activity that is most important right now. After you've organized and prioritized, pay attention to the task at hand and give it 110 percent until you're ready to move on to the next activity.

Stop what you're doing once every hour and ask yourself, "Am I making the most effective use of my time *right now?*"

The most important rule in time management is this: Don't let anyone tell you there is only one way to manage your time. Devise a system that works for you, and *keep it simple*. Simplicity is the key to effective time management; otherwise, we spend more time managing the process than we spend doing the activities. Keeping that in mind, here are a variety of tools and techniques you may want to incorporate into your own time management system.

The activity card

Every task you undertake during your work day should lead toward one goal—generating more sales. Some tasks lead more directly to this goal than others. In order to prioritize effectively, you need to analyze activities and evaluate their potential for generating sales. The card below is an activity-focuser, divided into three categories:

✓ **Prospecting for new business**. This is an "A" category, meaning that these are high priority activities for survival in sales. These activities (including telemarketing, canvassing, networking and getting referrals) should be done during prime selling hours: 8 a.m. to 6 p.m.

✓ **Growing and expanding your current base.** This "B" category includes all activities that enhance relationships and generate more business from your present clients. If you concentrate solely on getting new clients, the old ones will fall through the cracks. It's easy to take current customers for granted; however, it's five times harder to find a new customer than it is to keep one you already have. Activities in this list should also be done during prime selling hours.

✓ **Non-selling activities.** These are "C" activities that can be accomplished outside of prime selling hours. If you are a salesperson employed by a company, it might mean staying late some nights or taking work home. If you're an independent sales professional, it might mean hiring an assistant to help you get these tasks, such as writing reports and proposals, accomplished.

Sales activity card

(A) Prospecting for New Business	(B) Growing & Expanding Current Base	(C) Non-Selling Activities

✓Telemarketing
 	
✓Canvassing
 	
✓Mailing
  General
  Customized
 	
✓Networking
	✓Follow-up Calls
	  (on the phone &
	  in person)
	
	✓Referrals
	
	✓New Ideas
	
	✓Maintain
	  relationships
		✓Reports
		✓Proposals
		✓Administrative
		  work
		
		✓Follow-up letters
		✓Thank-yous
		
		✓General
		  paperwork

Design your own activity card that's customized to your selling environment. Review it first thing every morning to remind yourself of your daily priorities.

The to-do list

The to-do list is perhaps the simplest and most common time management tool of all, and it's also the most personal. Some people make a new list every day on 3 x 5 inch cards or Post-It Notes™. Some people prefer computerized lists and organizers (although it can be difficult to make additions or adjustments to your computerized list when you're on the road).

I like to keep mine running on a sheet of lined yellow paper and start a new list when I run out of room. That way, I have only one easy-to-carry sheet of paper to deal with. How you keep the list is not as important as the fact that you do keep one; the act of writing things down embeds them in your mind. Customize your list so that it's up-to-date, available for your daily use, and fits your personal style.

My list has three columns: Date, People to Call and Things to Do. When I begin a new list, I write down the people I need to call and the things I need to do in the appropriate columns. When I've made a call, I fill in the date next to the person's name, annotated so that I can remember what happened. If I left a message, my note will read "9/9, l/m" (I called on September 9 and left a message). Once the call is completed, the name is crossed off the list. As I complete the tasks in the Things to Do section, they are also crossed off the list. The example on the next page is what a new to-do list might look like.

Date completed: ___/___/___

DATE	PEOPLE TO CALL	THINGS TO DO
	John Smith 555-1234	Pick up copies of presentation packets
	**Conference call: me, Marty, Don	**Overnight materials to Myra Jones
	Kathryn Donelly re: possible meeting 555-5678	Make reservations for Chicago—plane and hotel
	Dan Tompkins 555-6971	Complete proposal for ABC Company
	George Atlas to confirm meeting w/VP sales 555-9006	Get D&B list of 100 top companies in 02300 zip code
	Elaine Bennet 555-7774	
	James Miller re proposal feedback 555-6633	

Here's what the list might look like three days later:

Date completed: ___/___/___

DATE	PEOPLE TO CALL	THINGS TO DO
9/8	John Smith 555-1234	Pick up copies of presentation packets
9/10	**Conference call: me, Marty, Don	**Overnight materials to Myra Jones
9/9, l/m	Kathryn Donelly re: possible meeting 555-5678	Make reservations for Chicago —plane and hotel
9/11	Dan Tompkins 555-6971	Complete proposal for ABC Company
9/9, w/c/b	**George Atlas to confirm meeting w/VP sales 555-9006	Get D&B list of 100 top companies in 02300 zip code
9/10	Elaine Bennet 555-7774	**Prepare presentation for Acme Buttons
9/9, 9/11	James Miller re proposal feedback 555-6633	Put together testimonial package for AMT present.
9/12, l/m	Hillary Johns 555-9921	**Letter & brochure to Steve at Lakeside
9/11	Arnold Leeds re new product intro	Make list of customer base & contact re new promotion

9/12	Jane Holland 555-4497	Order more business cards
9/10	**Frank Stone re 10/3 meeting with Jim 555-6693	
9/12, w/c/Fr	Philip Knight at Acme Button 555-2212	
9/12	Jim Akens 555-9988	
	Sam Mason 555-3331	
	Evelyn Falk XYZ Card Company 555-1213	

Here's what the new list, with leftover information transferred, might look like:

Date completed: ___/___/___

DATE	PEOPLE TO CALL	THINGS TO DO
9/9, lm	Kathryn Donnelly re: possible meeting 555-5678	Get D&B list of 100 top companies in 02300 zip code
9/12, lm	Hillary Johns 555-9921	Order more business cards
	Sam Mason 555-3331	
	Evelyn Falk XYZ Card Company 555-1213	

Copy this blank to-do sheet for your own use:

Date completed: ___/___/___

DATE	PEOPLE TO CALL	THINGS TO DO

The successful accomplishment of tasks breeds enthusiasm for continued success.

To-do checklist

✓ **Prepare your list the night before.** When you wake up, you're fresh and focused, and you know what needs to be done that day.

✓ **Prioritize your list.** Devise a system of marking high-priority items. You can categorize them using A, B, and C to denote high, middle and low priority; use a different color to denote the most important items; or mark high priority tasks with asterisks.

✓ **Check your to-do list several times during the day**. Do this to ensure that high priority tasks have been accomplished.

✓ **Cross off tasks as they are completed.**

✓ **Date your lists and keep them on file.** Look back through your lists every six months to a year. They may remind you of customers you want to get back in touch with. Looking back can also provide you with a realistic self-evaluation and progress report—it can be extremely helpful to look where you were a year ago, realize the progress you've made and recognize areas where you still need to improve.

Daily planners

It is your daily planner or appointment calendar, together with your to-do list, that keeps you on-track and focused during your selling day. This is how it works:

✓ On your to-do list for September 5 you have written "Call John Smith."

✓ You make the call and John Smith says, "We've had a breakdown at the plant. I can't talk to you now; call me back in two weeks."

✓ You cross John Smith's name off your to-do list.

✓ You take out your daily planner, turn to the page for September 19 and write "Call John Smith."

✓ On the evening of September 18, you check your planner for the next day's appointments (which now includes calling John Smith) and transfer them to your to-do list.

Using this back-and-forth system can help you avoid the three major scheduling faults:

1. Forgetting appointments.

2. Scheduling too much activity for one day.

3. Scheduling too little activity for one day.

Don't mistake movement for achievement. It's easy to keep yourself busy. The question is, busy doing what?

Daily planner checklist

✓ **Plan next week this week.** The time you spend on the phone today should result in scheduling appointments for next week or next month. This accomplishes three things:

1. It makes you appear busy and successful. Saying, "How's Tuesday, July 5th?" sounds better than, "I'm free this afternoon. How about if I pop right over?" (This may not be true if you've got a really hot prospect who's anxious to close. But even then it might be better to say, "I may be able to rearrange my schedule so that I can come by later today or first thing in the morning. Which would be better for you?")

2. There's a better chance of your customer having free time in a week or two than today or tomorrow.

3. It gives you something to look forward to. There's nothing better to keep you "pumped" than to know you've got a week of appointments—and opportunities—ahead of you.

✓ **Set up a territory map.** Break down your territory into key areas (especially if you're driving), and schedule all appointments in those areas for the same day or week. This will keep you concentrating on selling, not traveling. It also serves another purpose: The more sales you make within one area, the easier it is for word of mouth to spread about you and your product or service.

✓ **Cluster your tasks.** Organize your day so that you group similar activities together. For instance, suppose your tasks for the day are to make 10 phone calls, meet with two customers, write one proposal and four thank-you notes. The most effective schedule is make all the phone calls at once, set up appointments back-to-back and do the paperwork during non-selling hours.

✓ **Start out early and stay late.** Whether you're telemarketing or on the road, make appointments for 9:15 a.m. or 4:45 p.m. That way you can catch people before they get too busy or when they're winding down, and it will force you to put in a full day in between.

The Management Account Profile (MAP)

A basic element of a sales rep's job is to manage and track sales activity on an ongoing basis. The Management Account Profile (MAP) system is a practical visual aid to help salespeople focus on sales activity and receive immediate feedback. The MAP system results in increased sales activity, while pointing out areas that need improvement.

Hang a 2 x 3 foot cork board on the wall. Across the top of the board, make headings representing each stage of your company's typical sales cycle. Sample headings might be First Call, Presentation, Demonstration, Proposal, and Close. Your stages might be different, depending on your product, service and length of the sales cycle.

After you go on a first call to a prospect, come back to the office and fill out an account card with the name of the company, date of the call and—if applicable—product/dollar potential. The card is then placed on the MAP under the First Call column. As each stage in the sales cycle is completed, move the cards across the MAP until it reaches the closing stage.

One of the most important steps in the MAP system is recording the date each call is completed, illustrating how long a prospect has been in a specific column. Extra room should be left for cards in the first stage of the cycle. More activity should be generated here because there is a greater chance for cards to drop off in this early stage.

One of the most important benefits of the MAP system is the elimination of up-and-down months caused by lack of activity in a certain stage. When most of our time is spent in paperwork, we sometimes forget how critical prospecting activity can be for future business. The MAP board is a visual reminder showing us that the first stage may lack account cards.

Sample account card

ACCOUNT NAME *ABC Company*

Stage Completed	Date	Product
✓ Stage 1	5/2/91	XXX
___ Stage 2	___	
___ Stage 3	___	$ Potential
___ Stage 4	___	#15 K
___ Stage 5	___	

Once the first stage is completed, the card is then posted on the MAP under the First Call column. As each stage in the sale is completed, the account cards will move across the MAP until they end up in the closing stage. Additional columns could be added for service and follow-up.

Sample MAP boards: week one

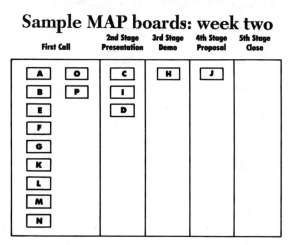

First Call	2nd Stage Presentation	3rd Stage Demo	4th Stage Proposal	5th Stage Close
A	H	J		
B	I			
C				
D				
E				
F				
G				

Week 1 in a 30-45 day sales cycle. Three accounts have already been moved to the second and third stages. The first stage has room for more cards since this is where most of the activity will be generated.

Sample MAP boards: week two

First Call		2nd Stage Presentation	3rd Stage Demo	4th Stage Proposal	5th Stage Close
A	O	C	H	J	
B	P	I			
E		D			
F					
G					
K					
L					
M					
N					

Here we see the sales rep has generated six more new accounts in the first stage and moved C,D,H,J accounts across the MAP.

Sample MAP boards: week three

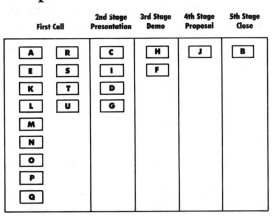

Additional prospects have been added to the first stage to compensate for the ones who have moved across the board.

Sample MAP boards: week eight

Jumping ahead to week eight, we see all the stages filled with activity, representing a highly productive sales representative in action. Note that the first stage should always have twice as many accounts as all the others.

117

Seeing is believing. MAP boards help you see your productivity and progress. They also help you determine the steps and stages you'll have to go through to reach your goal, while providing a visual representation of the steps you've already completed.

MAP board checklist

✓ **Be honest with yourself.** Every account posted on the MAP must be a qualified account—meaning that the account is going to make a buying decision in the next (insert your own sales cycle) days or months, either from you or your competitor.

✓ **Make sure that the first stage of the MAP always shows new activity being generated.** A sales rep who consistently has only two or three accounts in the first stage will see poor results in the final stage.

✓ **Use the MAP as an overview of your account activity.** It should be a constant visual reminder of where you stand in relation to where you need to be to achieve your goal.

✓ **Only move the account card across the board when a specific stage in MAP is completed.** This gives you a feeling of accomplishment, especially when you move the card from the proposal stage to the closing stage.

✓ **Write the date of each meeting on the account card.** This allows you to see how long your accounts have been sitting in each stage. This is especially helpful for your sales manager; he or she can monitor the board and take down accounts that are not qualified or strategize with you on how to move them across the MAP.

✓ **Post your monthly and yearly goals under the account board.** This will allow you to compare your sales activity with the goals you want to accomplish. Now you have a complete track to run on, and you can see the relationship between effort and results.

✓ **Review your board** and determine what activities will move each of your prospects to the next cycle.

Setting realistic and achievable goals

Earl Nightingale, one of the pioneers in the motivational tape industry and an inspiration to millions, defined success as the "...progressive realization of a worthy goal." In other words, it's the step-by-step activity, the striving towards a particular end, that really counts.

In sales, we set goals all the time. Too many times, however, we set goals based on what other people are doing. True goals are set against what you have previously accomplished and what you want to accomplish in the future. If you want to be the top salesperson in the company, don't think about beating last year's winner. Think about ways to improve your own performance. If you're constantly beating your own record, you'll work your way up to the top.

In order to work for you, goals must be realistic and achievable. To keep them that way, remember your ABC's.

- "A" goals are short-term, daily goals that you can cross off your to-do list once they're accomplished.

- "B" goals are monthly—tasks that can be accomplished or sales goals that can be reached within a 30-day period.

- "C" goals are long-term—what you want to have achieved within one, five or 10 years.

These lists are not set in stone. They should be revised and adapted frequently, so that you can look back at your lists and say, "This goal was not very productive; next time I'll try a different approach" or, "I set too many goals last month. I need to shift my time frame so that I'm able to carry out my plans."

The value of goal-setting is found in making plans and carrying them out. If your goal is to get a particular account, the specific steps you set up and follow are more valuable to you than the account itself. Once you have developed a workable plan, it's a guideline you can use to help you get other accounts. Goals help us to be proactive, focus on what needs to be done, and take necessary actions.

GOALS can be an acronym that explains how goals work:

1. **G**ather information.

2. **O**rganize.

3. **A**ct.

4. **L**ook back.

5. **S**et new goals.

✓ **Gather as much information as you can.**
Suppose your goal is to generate 10 new customers this month. It wouldn't be very efficient to simply open the phone book and start
making cold calls. Do your research. Here are
some examples:

- Make a list of the top 100 companies in your
territory (get this information from the library),
and use this list as your prospecting base.

- Call all your current accounts and ask for referrals. "Hi. I'm just calling to make sure that
everything is going well with our product's
performance. It is? That's great. By the way, I
was wondering if you might know of two or
three other companies in the area that could
benefit from our services?"

- Speak to service technicians or any other in-
dividuals in your company who have contact
with your accounts. They may be able to feed
you information about which accounts are potential upgrades.

✓ **Organize a step-by-step plan.** Make sure
your steps are in a logical sequence. Post your
plan on the wall. Look at it first thing in the
morning and at the end of the day. Keep a ver-
sion of it in your appointment book or wallet,
so that you're exposed to it all the time.

✓ **Action speaks louder than words.** This is
the most important step and the one that's
most underutilized. People usually give up on
goals before they've even started. They say,
"This is overwhelming. It's too hard to achieve."
The only antidote for this attitude is to dive

in, take one step at a time and to go for it. Pick up the phone. Start early. Call on accounts after hours. Experience is the best teacher.

✓ **Look back at the plan**. Are you on track? Do you need to change direction or add new steps? Ask yourself, "How much progress did I make? What can I do differently or more efficiently next time?" Evaluate any setbacks or obstacles you encountered. What lessons did you learn? Use this analysis to improve your goal-setting the next time.

✓ **Set new goals**. We're at our best when we're climbing, stretching and challenging ourselves. Goals pull us forward; they keep us focused and moving ahead. In sales, where rejection is an everyday occurrence, goals spark our enthusiasm and keep us motivated.

30-day action plan
(New Account Development)

1. Additional income I'd like to make this month

$_____

2. Number of sales it takes to make this much

_____

3. Number of presentations/appointments necessary to close the number of sales in Step #2

_____

✓ 4. Number of telemarketing/canvassing calls it takes to schedule the number of presentations or appointments in Step #3

_____   _____

Telemarketing/Canvass Calls			Presentations/Appointments	
	Plan	Actual	Plan	Actual
Week 1				
Week 2				
Week 3				
Week 4				

Total New Sales/Accounts: _____

Total Volume/Revenue: _____

Total Commission: _____

We all need long-term goals to keep us going during short-term setbacks.

Goal-setting checklist

✓ **Write down your goals and the steps it will take to achieve them.** This takes the goal out of the realm of fantasy and puts it into the realm of possibility. It gives you a realistic picture of what it will take to achieve your objective, and it breaks down an "impossible" goal into small, achievable steps.

✓ **Be flexible and remain realistic.** There's no such thing as an unachievable goal. It's just that we run out of time. Remember that goals are only guidelines; they're meant to be changed as we put our plans into action in the real world. Leave yourself room and time to make discoveries. You may find new ways to get to your goal—ways you never even knew existed.

✓ **When setting goals, ask yourself these five questions:**

1. Where am I now?
2. Where do I want to end up?
3. Why do I want to go there?
4. What's the best way to get there?
5. What do I expect to be, get or have happen when I arrive?

Write your answers down, and keep them somewhere accessible so that you can review, revise and rewrite them as necessary.

✓ **Make a list of the major benefits** you will receive from achieving your goals. Review the list often as an incentive to keep yourself moving forward.

✓ **Write your most important goals down on a small card.** Carry it in your wallet or stick it on your refrigerator. Ask yourself every day, "What can I do today to get closer to my goal?"

How to set up a war room

When the top brass are planning their campaigns and battle strategies during war time, they set up a special meeting room where the walls are lined with charts, maps and objectives to be reached—the war room. Everything is in plain view so that immediate assessments can be made.

You can set up your own war room—a space where you can, with one glance, know what you've already accomplished and what's left to be done. It should also be a place where you know you mean business. As you look around you can say, "Here's what needs to be done today." This is the place to gather yourself together, focus and get things done.

You become what you think about.

Remind yourself constantly that you are successful, and you're on your way to being even better. Set up your environment so that it is an area of positive encouragement. Put your MAP board on the wall, and hang a list of your goals nearby. Keep testimonials, letters of recognition and awards where you can see them or get to them easily. This is not so that you can brag to other people, but so that you can walk into this space and be surrounded by tangible reminders of accomplishment.

War room checklist

✓ **Set up the space as it works best for you.** Some people work well in clutter. Some must have a place for everything and everything in its place. No matter what your style is—or whether you're working out of a large corporate office or a corner of your dining room—arrange the space so that it's a reminder of what you've already accomplished and a guide to where you want to go.

✓ **Let your past inspire your future.** It's not enough to set up a gallery of past achievements. Use these reminders to say, "I did it before; I can do it again." Remember all the rejections you encountered along the way, and how hard you worked to achieve your goals. Let these memories serve as reminders not to give up or get discouraged.

✓ **Review your goals periodically.** Set both short-term and long-term goals, and review them every week or every month. Sometimes an amazing synergy will occur—you'll suddenly realize how two seemingly unrelated (or even opposite) goals can come together and move you forward in an even more exciting direction.

✓ **Remember, you become what you think about.** Your thoughts are the power centers of your life. Keep your goals in front of you so they become part of you, as if by osmosis. Surround yourself with ideals of achievement. Read books by and about those who inspire you. Listen to audio tapes. Make one of your goals to surround yourself with positive, achievement-oriented people. Believe in your ability to achieve.

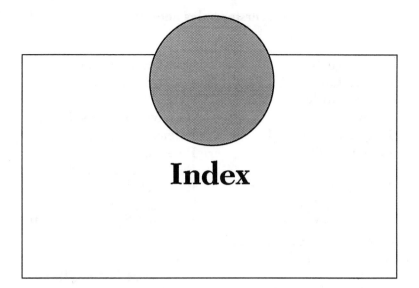

Index

Account cards, 115, 118
Action, 17, 19-20, 121-123
Activity card, 103-105
Announcement cards, 34-35
Arguing, with
    customers, 86-87
Attitude, 9-15, 41-42

Body language, 60-61

Closing, 89-93
Cold calling, 24-28
Communication,
    maintaining, 98
Customer base, 38-45
Customers
    keeping, 44-45
    needs, 73-75, 91
    portfolio, 45-48
    selling for you, 45-48
    tough, 84-86

Daily planners, 111-114
Demonstrations, 79-80
Dun & Bradstreet, 51, 53

Enthusiasm, 9, 41-42, 75-76
Eye contact, making, 77

Failure, 11, 16-19
Fear, 16-19
Feedback, 43
Follow-up, 43, 62-63,
    95-99

Goals, setting,
    119-124, 126

Humor, using, 24-25

I Dare You!, 13
Information, 27, 121

Language
  bad habits, 78
  descriptive, 78
  vivid, 77
List, to-do, 105-111
Listening, 60-62, 83

Management Account
  Profile (MAP), 39,
    114-119, 125
Mistakes, learning from, 23
Motivation, 7-20

Needs analysis, 49-63
Networking, 14, 33-37
Notes, taking, 54, 58, 67

Objections, handling,
  27, 32, 47, 81-87
Organizing, 102, 121
Overnight success,
  myth of, 12-13

Persistence, 10-11
Pitfalls, sales, 17-18
Practice, 15-16
Preparation, 17, 19-20, 71
Presentations, 65-80
Prioritizing, 102, 111
Product, belief in, 23
Promises,
  delivering, 43-44, 99
Prospecting, 21-48

Questions, asking,
  54-62, 69, 83

Reference sources, 52-53
References, 46-48
Rejection, 22
Relationships, 22, 37
Research, 50-53
Respect, 40-41
Role models, positive, 14-15

Sales
  success factors, 18-20
  pitfalls, 17-18
Schedule, for follow-up
  calls, 98
Solutions, 84, 92
Surveys, 39, 96-97

Telemarketing, 28-33
Testimonials, 45-48, 76, 87
Thank-you notes, 35-37, 98
Time management, 101-126
To-do list, 105-111
Top-down selling, 25

Voice, using, 77-78

War room, 125-126